Paradise Transformed: Los Angeles During the Second World War

Arthur C. Verge
El Camino College

Library of Congress Catalog Card Number: 93-78610

ISBN 0–7872–0531–1

Printed in the United States of America
10 9 8 7 6 5 4 3

❑ Dedication ❑

To–Art and Margie Verge,
Jeff, Suzanne and Christopher Lloyd Peak,
Annette and Louie Chao, and of course,
Mark and Patrick Verge, without whose love and
support this book could not have been written.

❑ Acknowledgments ❑

In the preparation of this book I have incurred many scholarly debts of gratitude to numerous individuals and institutions that have made this work possible. I am indebted to the members of the Department of History at the University of Southern California. During my years of graduate training there, members of the department continually went beyond the call of duty to assist me in a wide range of endeavors. Their devotion to excellence in teaching and research has greatly impacted my life and career. I am particularly indebted to Professor Frank Mitchell under whose guidance and direction this work was begun. The epitome of a gentleman and scholar, Professor Mitchell remains a testament to what is right with American higher education. I also had the good fortune to work for Professor John A. Schutz, whose wit, wisdom, and counsel continue to sustain me. I also wish to deeply thank professors Terry Seip, Ed Perkins, Roger Dingman, Mauricio Mazon, Doyce Nunis, Paul Knoll, Lloyd Moote, and Larry Berg. Each of these individuals played an instrumental part in shaping my professional career as an historian.

The work herein has also been influenced by the teachings and counsel given by professors Alex DeConde, Alex Callow, and Fred Viehe of the University of California at Santa Barbara, and Richard Ruetten of San Diego State University. It has been my good fortune to have had each as an instructor of history, and their love of the subject seems to have rubbed off. Unquestionably my work has been deeply influenced and inspired by the scholastic writings and personal encouragement given by both Professors Gerald Nash and Roger Lotchin. Their trailblazing works in the field of the American Urban West in conjunction with their substantial help and support for young historians will serve to influence students of American history for generations to come.

My gratitude for support in this endeavor especially extends to the following: For their extensive reading and corrections of this manuscript I wish to greatly thank Frank Mitchell, John Schutz, Terry Seip, Jon Nielson, Thom Armstrong, Cheryl Armstrong, Gabriel Meyer, Bud Grantham, Mike Engh, and Howard Shorr. Their suggestions, critical comments, and assistance in so many ways have left their mark on a much improved manuscript. Special thanks to my sister Suzanne Peak for her work on the book's bibliography and to Dr. Jon Nielson for his assistance in compiling the book's index. A special thank you to Suzanne Brown, Joe Sikorra, Mike King, and Dwayne Hayden for their help with the book's cover.

I also am indebted for the kinship with my friends of the Los Angeles History Group at the Huntington Library. Our shared work under the direction of Fr. Mike Engh, Howard Shorr, and Martin Ridge has dramatically expanded the field of Los Angeles history. Special thanks to Gloria Ricci Lothrop, Don and Nadine Hata, Martin Schiesl, and Andrew Rolle, whose advice and essential research I often find myself drawing upon.

For the substance of friendship, I need look no further than my colleagues at El Camino College. One could not ask for a nicer grouping of individuals. Their true commitment to excellence in teaching while pursuing scholarly objectives remains a special inspiration for me. I also wish to thank El Camino College for its unswerving institutional support of this project. The school's financial support has allowed me to share my research at the California Studies Conference in Sacramento, California and the Western Historian Association Meeting at Yale University. I am also indebted for their award of a generous Scholarly Research grant that has enabled me to complete this work.

Of the many friendships I have been blessed to share in I wish to warmly acknowledge Jim Kraft and Thom Armstrong, two members of the historical profession who have always kept me going despite the inevitable obstacles one encounters in researching and writing a book. I also cherish the time I spent with my "partners in crime" at graduate school which include Rosa Bettencourt, Mark Konnert, Ron Love, and Phil Pope.

I also wish to express the deep gratitude I have for Los Angeles County Lifeguards, an organization with which I have been associated for more than twenty years. Many of the happiest days of my life have been spent working on the beaches of Los Angeles. While the profession of lifesaving is often misperceived by the public at large, I am very proud that I was able to attend graduate school by working as an ocean lifeguard. Lifeguarding also enabled to me to travel and to see the world through a wide variety of ocean competitions. Saving lives from a capricious and too often treacherous ocean transcends international boundaries and creates bonds of friendship that endure the test of time. Thus to my fellow salt water colleagues, especially those who have suffered permanently disabling injuries, I say thanks for having been there. My life has been particularly blessed with lots of joy and laughter. While much of it has been provided by my students, fellow faculty members, and lifeguard colleagues, special thanks go to Dr. Eric Shargo, Mark (Shecky) Samet, Phil and Cindee Topar, Tony and Lynn Deluca, Dave Kastigar, Mike and Theresa Frazier, Rich and Theresa Piedmont, Ray and Cathy Yonke,

Jeanne and Gordon Flynn, George and Nancy McInnis, Dan and Shirley Cragin, Dick and Helen Vasak. Special thanks also to my relatives John and Lori Glass and Rosemary and Steve Macleod, in whose homes I have stayed on what was often intended to be a research trip. I also wish to thank the friends with whom I've shared long runs, walks and talks. Those times are cherished for clearing the mind and sharing insights into the meaning of life. Of great importance to me has also been the roles of swim coaches John Joseph, Terry Palma, Stu Blumkin, Gregg Wilson, Clay Evans, Corey Stanbury, Bonnie and Mark Spivey. All of these have given unceasingly of themselves and in the process of their work have taught thousands of swimmers under their tutelage the value of going the distance.

For this book I owe a large debt to numerous individuals who have shared their wartime experiences with me. In particular my father, who before being "shipped out" aboard the YO 45 to the naval battle of Catalina Island, spent the war years here in Los Angeles. A partial list of others who shared their memories of wartime Los Angeles include, Opel and Jack Winter, Virginia Spurgin, Bob Crawford, Mrs. Fredrick Koehner, Bruce Fitzpatrick, Bob Moore, John A. Schutz, Bob Walthour, and combat veterans, Ray Acevado, Archie Morrison, Gene Verge, John Joseph, Charlie Dunbar, and Chuck Spurgin. I also wish to acknowledge my uncle Lt. Cmdr. Rob Costello, who before being moved with the fleet to Pearl Harbor spent many languid days in pre-war Los Angeles. His memories of those times, as well as his painful memories of his experiences at Pearl Harbor, Iwo Jima and Okinawa, have helped to put the massive production effort of the homefront in clear perspective.

My gratitude also extends to the staffs of the many libraries and archives I visited in the course of researching and writing this book. Particularly helpful was the assistance rendered by the staffs of the Huntington Library, the Los Angeles City Archives, and the staffs of the university libraries of the University of California at Los Angeles, the University of Southern California, and California State University Dominquez Hills. In obtaining photographs for the book I deeply appreciate the great work of Dacy Taub at the University of Southern California's Los Angeles Regional History Center and Joan Sewald of Los Angeles Department of Airports. Staffs of the U.S. Naval Institute, National Archives and the Library of Congress further made photo illustrations possible.

The greatest source of inspiration for this book remains my family and in particular, my mother and father. No one could be more blessed.

For any errors of fact and judgment which appear on the pages contained herein, I assume full responsibility.

Arthur C. Verge

El Camino College

Torrance, California

❑ Contents ❑

❑ Introduction ❑

"It was the best of times, it was the worst of times."

—Charles Dickens

"The War." Two simple words that are often still uttered with deep emotion. For millions of Americans, the Second World War was the most transformative event of their lives. In the swirl of the most devastating conflict in human history, many Americans found their participation in the war effort to have had a redemptive quality upon their lives. In sharp contrast to the faith shattering years of the Great Depression, many Americans emerged from the war with a renewed sense of confidence in themselves and in the nation's democratic institutions. The popular description of World War 2 as the "Last Good War" gives testament to the conflict's mixed legacy of national unity and shared purpose in the face of hundreds of thousands of wounded and war dead.

The war's mixed legacy also extended into the nation's cities. While bread lines gave way to crowded factory gates, municipal authorities often found themselves contending with such "boom town" ills as congested streets, overwhelmed sewer systems, housing shortages, rising crime rates, and public health epidemics to name but a few of the war's difficult legacies. Yet, the war also spelled prosperity for many urban centers as aging, rust ridden factories gave way to new modernized manufacturing plants, whose design and assembly technologies were often the envy of the world. In addition, the industrial production demands of the war created record numbers of new jobs that served to lift millions of Americans out of poverty and into a middle-class existence.

While the impact of the Second World War was felt throughout the American homefront, no other American urban center was as transformed by the war as was Los Angeles. Once perceived as a distant western outpost, isolated and separated by 3,000 miles from the nation's industrialized East, Los Angeles, bolstered by massive federal defense spending, emerged in the war as an industrial giant whose production of vital defense goods, such as warships and planes, helped turn the war in the Allies favor. Further, the city's world renowned entertainment industry played a pivotal role in shaping and maintaining the nation's morale behind the Allied war effort.

Los Angeles paid for its rise to industrial greatness largely at the expense of its environment. Many of the region's scenic orange groves fell victim to bulldozers, whose owners then built instant suburbs that became known as "stucco ghettos." Picturesque Santa Monica Bay fared little better as it became a wartime dumping ground for raw sewage and industrial waste. The city's air quality, too, deteriorated, becoming so bad that by 1943 the words "smoke" and "fog" were combined into the word "smog" to explain the new thick brown haze that was covering the city's skies.

Wartime Los Angeles was also pained by acute racism, most notable of which was the widespread support for the forced removal and internment of the city's large Japanese-American community. Blacks and Hispanics, too, suffered, struggling under the burden of racially restrictive housing covenants, widespread job discrimination, and segregated public facilities such as pools and beaches. Yet, the war also provided new opportunities for women and minorities. Access to jobs in the previously closed high paying defense industries helped to encourage a renewed and stronger civil rights movement.

Despite the city's wartime trials and tribulations, Los Angeles emerged from the Second World War as the leading urban center of the American West. Once perceived as a distant western outpost, California's "City of Angels" was, by 1943, home to one in forty Americans. This book explores the war's impact on Los Angeles' growth and development. Like the war itself, it is a story of pain and triumph.

Los Angeles on the Eve of War

1

On the eve of the Second World War Los Angeles was moving from its rural past into its urban future. Physically, large open spaces and vacant city lots checkered much of the Los Angeles basin. From the coastal suburbs of Hermosa Beach and Redondo Beach, where dirt roads and small farms were commonplace, one could gaze northeast over the basin plain and clearly see Los Angeles City Hall in the distance. Across the basin, in areas east of the burgeoning downtown, Los Angeles residents could drive their cars along quiet roads adjacent to large tracts of farm land. As one Angeleno who lived in La Canada Flintridge recalled, "up until World War 2 this was all orange groves and grape vineyards. You could ride a horse for miles with nothing in sight."[1]

Los Angeles, the city known today as the "freeway capital of the world," did not have a single mile of freeway in 1939.[2] Visitors to its environs often described prewar Los Angeles in romantic terms deeming it "the land of sunshine," "a tourist's Mecca," or quite simply, "small town Los Angeles."[3] Several professional surveyors of the region's prewar industrial and manufacturing capacity concurred, deeming the future metropolis, "a small plant town."[4]

The physical appearance of prewar Los Angeles, however, proved to be as deceptive as one of the region's carefully crafted movie sets. For beneath the small town veneer was a large and blossoming economy. As early as 1937, Los Angeles was successfully competing with the nation's more established eastern seaboard cities. That year, it ranked third among American cities in the number of manufacturing establishments and fifth in the value of manufactured output.[5] By 1939, Los Angeles County led the nation in the number of predominant industries, ranking first in the production of aircraft, motion pictures, sportswear, oil well equipment, and food products.[6]

As the city's population approached one and a half million residents in 1939, making it the nation's fifth largest metropolitan area, its mayor, Fletcher Bowron, proudly asserted that, "Los Angeles is coming into its own." Brushing aside remarks from such detractors as Sinclair Lewis, who once characterized Los Angeles as "the retreat of all failures," the mayor in his 1939 New Year's Day address pointed to the region's burgeoning economy and boasted, "No longer will persons from other parts of the state or other sections of the country deride Los Angeles as an overgrown village, the center of scandals and sensations, the place of incubation for crackpot ideas, economic or otherwise."[7]

The Depression years proved pivotal in shaping Los Angeles on the eve of the Second World War. While the city suffered from large reductions in municipal services, mass unemployment, and inadequate public relief programs, Los Angeles nonetheless weathered the Great Depression better than many of its municipal counterparts. City government avoided bankruptcy through a variety of belt tightening measures, several of which forced the citizenry to look beyond City Hall to Washington D.C. for economic assistance. Subsequent federal aid had an important two-fold effect. First, it lessened Los Angeles' historic feeling of separation and isolation from the more industrialized eastern half of the country. Second, it produced a dramatic shift in political party affiliation as the majority of Angelenos turned away from Hoover Republicanism, to embrace much of the Democratic party's New Deal.[8]

Despite the numerous ill effects left behind in the Depression's wake, most notably in the areas of housing, health, race and ethnic relations, Los Angeles emerged from the Depression decade matured. Historic dependence on real estate speculation and tourism waned as Angelenos searched for greater economic stability. Local civic leaders in particular paid increasing attention to solving the problems of the region's burgeoning industrial base.

The city's growing economic vitality in 1939 can be largely traced to far-sighted investment of eastern manufacturers, who were setting up branch plant operations in Southern California. Eastern manufacturer's including R.C.A. Victor, Firestone Tire, Dow Chemical, Ford Motor, and Bethlehem Steel all built plants in Los Angeles. The region's enticements proved abundant. Los Angeles offered manufacturers a pro-business atmosphere, a near perfect climate, large tracts of vacant affordable land, a rapidly growing population, and strong local petroleum industry that offered inexpensive power. Further, the city's strategic Pacific coast location and port facilities served as an ideal commercial and manufacturing center for exporting goods to Pacific Rim nations.[9]

The optimism that reigned in Los Angeles on New Year's Day 1939 seemed tempered only by international news stories that signalled serious challenges to world peace. Readers of the New Year's Day edition of the Los Angeles *Times* learned that the United States was angrily protesting

Japanese attempts to establish "special privileges" in war torn China, and that in Nazi Germany, nine new decrees against Jews had become official law. In truth, the stories of a world in turmoil seemed remote to most people living in Los Angeles. Like the vast majority of Americans, the citizens of Los Angeles overwhelmingly supported neutrality as the foundation of American foreign policy.

But as the world rapidly changed in 1939, so did public opinion. The quickening pace of German and Japanese aggression in the early months of 1939 alerted Americans that legalistic pronouncements of neutrality would not be enough to ward off the threat of a global war. However, even as late as Germany's brazen invasion of Poland on September 1, 1939, the United States found itself woefully unprepared, ranking a deplorable nineteenth on the scale of world military powers. American military aviation was in especially poor shape given that the majority of its planes were outdated for use in combat.[10] From this turbulent scenario and military inadequacy, Los Angeles emerged as one of the world's leading defense producers.

The growing field of aviation was attracted to Los Angeles early on. Local business boosters were able to sell Southern California to the embryotic industry through promises of investment, technological assistance, and a large available work force. Further, as late as 1939, the manufacturing capacity of Los Angeles was still relatively underdeveloped.[11] In that year, only 5.4 percent of Los Angeles County's total population was employed in manufacturing, as compared to a national average of 15.4 percent found in the nation's thirty-two leading production centers.[12] Thus, the city, with its cheap land, conducive weather and business climate, was able to attract a large segment of the aviation industry to the greater Los Angeles area. Once here, many of the pioneer aviators encouraged other like minded souls to migrate west. The newcomers were particularly enamored of the region's geographical attributes, the Pacific Ocean, near by mountains and lakes, a large desert, all of which were ideal as proving grounds to test new planes.

The Depression years had not been kind to the aircraft industry. Most aviation companies went bankrupt. Adding to the industry's woes was the passage of the Vinson-Trammel Act in 1936. Passed by Congress because of public disdain for the profits made by defense manufacturers in World War 1, the law limited the profits of aircraft companies to a set minimum percentage of a defense contract. Also discouraging production was the fact that Los Angeles aircraft manufacturers were wary of military contracts. A short war or a sudden termination of a military contract could quickly bankrupt a company. Further, aircraft plant owners chafed at the high start-up costs that military orders imposed.

The aircraft industry in 1937 was still experimental, and the production of commercial aircraft remained a risky venture as well. Glen Martin, one of aviation's great innovators and designers, warned his former engineer, a young Donald Douglas, that there was "no better way of going broke than building commercial planes in Southern California."[13]

In 1937, airframe and related manufacture in Los Angeles was considered a minor industry, employing only five percent of the region's industrial workers. That same year, however, was one in which the dark ominous clouds of war thickened over Europe. In response, Congress began to modify its isolationist position. The same Congress that a year earlier had imposed profit margins on defense manufacturers was, by 1938, looking for incentives to increase warplane production. The real savior for Los Angeles aircraft manufacturers, though, came from Britain and France. Fearing impending war they willingly paid in advance for their warplane orders. In June 1938, Lockheed Aircraft of Burbank received one of the region's first substantial foreign orders—a British order for 200 warplanes.

A Frenchman weeps as German soldiers march into Paris on June 14, 1940. (Photograph courtesy of the National Archives)

By 1939, Congress had formally approved of this on going "cash and carry" program. This was particularly beneficial in that it gave aircraft manufacturers in Los Angeles the opportunity to safely expand their plants by producing already paid for war planes. Upon formal adoption of the "cash and carry" program, a torrent of foreign military orders flowed into the Los Angeles region. British and French purchases by the end of the first nine months of 1939 accounted for 71 percent of the value of American aircraft exports. By 1940, the dollar value of aircraft exports represented 84 percent of all total sales made by the U.S. aircraft industry.[14]

Foreign money enabled the Los Angeles aircraft industry to expand without greatly raising the ire of American taxpayers, and perhaps more importantly, the large orders encouraged important changes in manufacturing techniques that would be indispensable when the war effort became full-scale. Britain, the aircraft industry's largest customer, for example, insisted on standardization of its planes and would often have the same

While many Angelenos are able to bask in sunshine, stoic Britons are forced to contend with nightly German air raids over England in the summer of 1940. Pictured here is the burning result of one such raid over Sheffield, England. (Photograph courtesy of the National Archives)

model produced by several manufacturers. The end result was an increase in cooperation between various companies, and the development of highly sophisticated mass production techniques.[15]

The test of these recently acquired skills came in May of 1940, when President Franklin D. Roosevelt made his famous request that the aircraft industry prepare to turn out 50,000 planes a year. Given their initial experience in filling foreign defense orders, local aircraft manufacturers believed the goal possible. As European and American defense orders flowed in, local aircraft manufacturers greatly expanded their operations. Work shifts were added as backlogs continued to increase. Douglas Aircraft of Santa Monica was so busy that it became one of the nation's first defense manufacturers to operate around the clock, seven days a week.[16]

The industry's growth was dramatic. Aircraft employment in Los Angeles soared from 15,930 at the end of 1938, to over 120,000 when the United States entered the war in December 1941. The aircraft industry went from employing five percent of all the industrial workers in Los Angeles County in 1937, to employing more than 40 percent in 1942.[17] The aircraft industry in Los Angeles was not the sole beneficiary of America's defense build-up. Since World War 1 the area's shipbuilding industry had been inactive, but as defense orders mounted, the shipyards of Los Angeles embarked on a remarkable expansion program. The industry, which averaged 1,000 employees in 1939, grew to 22,000 by October 1941. Literally starting from scratch, the shipbuilding industry of Los Angeles busily constructed and refitted vessels that would be critical to the Allied war effort.[18]

The influx of defense orders after 1939 caused the Los Angeles industrial area to grow at a startling pace, earning it distinction as the nation's fastest growing region.[19] Not everyone was pleased with the unprecedented growth. Local writer Sarah Comstock complained, "Towns do not develop here, they are instantly created, synthetic communities of a strangely artificial world."[20]

The rapid industrial growth caused numerous problems, especially for those working in the region's agriculture industry. Large portions of scenic citrus groves that employed thousands in harvesting, sorting, packing, and shipping of fruit were quickly bought up by real estate speculators, who correctly sensed that the flat, water-accessible land would be ideal for urban development.

While Los Angeles farm land literally lost ground to urbanization, industrialization, and population growth, the agriculture industry as a whole remained surprisingly resilient. Due to the size and value of its principal crops, including citrus, walnuts, and vegetables, as well as dairy and poultry products, Los Angeles, prior to and during the Second World War, remained the nation's most important agricultural county.[21]

The size and strength of Los Angeles' agriculture industry proved particularly beneficial in feeding the region's burgeoning population. Although Los Angeles did not experience the tremendous demographic growth of the "boom twenties," the region's population still increased by more than 20 percent during the 1930's. Between 1930 and 1940 the city of Los Angeles experienced the second largest population increase (258,744) among all American cities, save New York (449,813).[22]

By 1940 the population of the City of Los Angeles was 1,504,792, and greater Los Angeles County was 2,785,643.[23] Characteristically, Los Angeles in 1940 was populated by a predominantly white, adult, urban-oriented population.[24] In the city, for example, 93.5 percent of the populace was classified as white by the 1940 census. Notably Hispanics, whom the 1940 census takers classified as white, made up at least 10 percent of the Los Angeles population.[25] Moreover by 1940 more than half of the black population of California was living in Los Angeles, comprising 4.2 percent of the city's population and 2.7 percent of the county's.[26]

Unfortunately for new arrivals, Los Angeles on the eve of war did not offer immediate economic relief for those victimized by the Great Depression. Despite increasing employment opportunities in 1940, unemployment still remained relatively high. Within the city, more than 14 percent of the residents remained unemployed. In large part this can be attributed to the tendency of migration to outrun employment opportunities. Particularly hard hit in 1940 were large numbers of blacks migrating to Los Angeles from the Jim Crow South. Several defense manufacturers remained opposed to their being hired, and partly because of this, black unemployment averaged 26.6 percent in 1940.[27] Finding employment was not the only problem migrants faced. The city itself proved utterly confusing. In 1940, Los Angeles was an intertwining mosaic of 45 incorporated and 60 unincorporated communities which varied in size from Los Angeles' municipal population of 1,504,277, to West Covina's 850. Real estate speculation and poor planning gave way to urban sprawl, and the city by 1940 had lost its distinct center.[28] Humorists no longer talked of Los Angeles as "six suburbs," but instead described it, "as one hundred communities in search of a city."

However, "run-away" suburbs and speculative subdivisions did have positive benefits for migrants in that decentralization encouraged building in outlying areas. As orange groves and cow pastures fell to builders, Los Angeles was able to escape, prior to the outbreak of war, the serious housing shortages that beset many other defense production areas of the nation. Yet, as the city expanded away from its center the problems of public transportation increased.

Since 1895, Los Angeles had an interurban streetcar system. By the late 1930s, the Pacific Electric Railway System, with its fondly remembered "Big Red Cars," covered a transportation network of nearly eleven thousand miles.[29] However, the system wasn't designed to carry large numbers of defense workers to and from the war plants. Large-scale abandonment of the "noisy, uncomfortable, ugly, often badly lighted" railway cars was done in favor of the automobile. This only added to the city's increasing traffic congestion woes. Los Angeles *Times* reporter, Ed Ainsworth, complained in 1938 that Los Angeles was becoming atrophied because of its traffic problems.[30] Quickly the growing competition between automobiles and streetcars for the control of public roadways became a major issue. On the eve of the war the automobile was clearly winning the battle. In 1940, for example, an estimated 80 percent of all passenger miles traveled in Los Angeles were done by car.[31] Moreover, there were more cars in Los Angeles in 1939 than in all the states of the Union, save six.[32]

Studies of the region's traffic congestion found that most of the problem stemmed from Los Angeles' attempt to accommodate slower, local traffic along with that which was faster and more distance-oriented, on the same roadways. What was needed, local traffic planners concluded, was a transportation network of roads that would be for the exclusive use of motor vehicles. This network, as they planned, would be free of traffic lights and grade crossings. Support for the rapid transit network came from local city planners who argued that without it, Los Angeles would become a high-density city. A "freeway system," they pointed out, would encourage the city to spread away from a potentially overcrowded nucleus.[33]

In 1940, construction crews completed building the city's first freeway. It linked the downtown civic center with Pasadena.[34] At the very same time, sharp declines in ridership and profits forced the Pacific Electric Railway to abandon outright many of its railway franchises. Only the war effort, with its curtailment of gasoline and rubber products, provided a temporary reprieve for the system's eventual demise.[35]

Los Angeles' growing reliance on the automobile also had a strong impact on the local petroleum industry.

Historically, the petroleum industry had been critical to the early development of Los Angeles. Large oil discoveries in the early 1920s facilitated the region's rapid growth, offering fuel for industry and private use at inexpensive prices.[36] While production dropped from a peak of approximately 700,000 barrels a day in 1923, to 300,000 barrels a day in 1941, the continued revenue of more than 200 million dollars a year substantially aided Los Angeles' economic growth.[37]

Ironically, Los Angeles' best foreign customer on the eve of war was Japan. In 1939, nearly 40 percent of Los Angeles' exported oil went to Japan.[38] Concerned that much of this oil was being used by the Japanese to fuel their war machine in Asia, President Roosevelt issued a presidential order on August 1, 1940, that barred the export of high octane gasoline and tetraethyl lead to Japan.

F.D.R.'s order received strong support from two unusual areas, the oil industry and the United States Navy. The oil industry supported the order since domestic demand for fuel products had increased by nearly 20 percent since 1939. In particular, aviation fuel was in short supply. By 1940, the need was so great that Donald Douglas of Douglas Aircraft constructed his own oil refinery to produce 100 plus octane fuel. Both Standard and Union Oil companies followed suit, investing millions to meet the demands of the military's growing reliance on airpower.

The United States Navy, and in particular naval authorities in Los Angeles, supported the order because Japanese tankers in Los Angeles were handling an average of 60,000 barrels of oil a day. It was feared that these tankers, which were regularly coming in and out of Los Angeles Harbor, had been spying on the still home-ported Pacific Fleet.

Ironically, Los Angeles had been chosen the home port of the Pacific Fleet in 1919 because of increasing tensions between the United States and Japan. A very concerned President Woodrow Wilson, fearful of an expansionist Japan in Asia, had ordered a transfer of 200 warships to the West Coast. Naval authorities considered the Port of San Diego too shallow for the fleet's largest ships and, therefore, selected the Ports of San Pedro (Los Angeles Harbor) and Long Beach in San Pedro Bay as the fleet's new home.[39] By 1939, San Pedro Bay was home to one of the world's greatest naval armadas. Included in this fleet were the aircraft carriers *Lexington* and *Saratoga*, and the battleships, *Arizona*, *California*, *Colorado*,

A languid day in San Pedro (1939) as crew members from the pictured battleships, *Arizona, New Mexico,* and *Mississippi* compete in a sail boat race. Shown taking an early lead is the team from the *Arizona* (B 39). (Photograph courtesy of the United States Naval Institute)

Idaho, *Maryland*, *Mississippi*, *Nevada*, *New Mexico*, *Oklahoma*, *Pennsylvania*, and *West Virginia*.[40]

As tensions mounted between Japan and the United States in the late 1930s, Japanese spying on the American Pacific fleet increased. Using surveillance-equipped fishing boats, Japanese agents operating out of Guaymas, Mexico carefully shadowed and monitored the Pacific Fleet's off-shore operations. In 1939, Japanese agents in Los Angeles successfully bribed a former Pacific Fleet sailor to spy on the fleet. The sailor, wearing his old uniform, boarded several warships from which he stole several naval codebooks. Although he was eventually apprehended, the stolen materials had already been passed to the Japanese consulate by the time American authorities broke the case. The spying successes of the Japanese prompted naval authorities in Los Angeles to institute strict security measures to protect the fleet.[41]

While American intelligence agents contended with foreign espionage in San Pedro Bay, state and local police officials were fighting their own battle in adjacent Santa Monica Bay. In 1939, Santa Monica Bay was home to several gambling ships whose colorful owners and shady finances prompted fears of an East Coast mobster takeover of Los Angeles. Attracted by the region's growing wealth and population, East Coast mobsters such as "Bugsy" Siegal openly moved to Los Angeles in a clear attempt to gain control of the city's rampant vice operations.

Sensing that a shutdown of the gambling ships would signal an end to the city's previous tolerance of such vice, battle lines were drawn in the summer of 1939. The main target of law enforcement officials was "Admiral of the Fleet," mobster Tony Cornero.

Admiral Tony's pride and joy was the gambling ship *Rex,* located directly three miles off the Santa Monica pier. Claiming that his ship operated in international waters, and was therefore immune from state and local prosecution, Tony collected handsomely from those who gambled

With fire hoses at the ready, the crew of Tony Cornero's gambling ship *Rex* prepares to stave off another boarding attempt by law enforcement officials in the colorful "Battle of Santa Monica Bay," August, 1939. (Photograph courtesy of the University of Southern California's Regional History Center.)

away thousands of dollars a day aboard his ship.[42] Cornero's continued and open defiance of legal proceedings against him prompted California's Attorney General, Earl Warren, to take action.

What became known as the "Battle of Santa Monica Bay" began with an afternoon police raid on the gambling ships on August 2, 1939. To the delight of crowds watching from the Santa Monica pier, Tony's crew aboard the *Rex* fought off attempted boardings by law enforcement officials with fire hoses. The entertaining battle lasted for eight days. When it was finally over, the tired but somewhat heroic, "Admiral Tony" was booked at the Santa Monica police station. Asked by the booking sergeant to give his occupation, the bitter Cornero snarled, "Mariner, Goddamnit!"[43]

The shutting down of the gambling ships signalled another important victory in a growing war against organized crime in Los Angeles. In 1938, the city was rocked with the news that the head of the Los Angeles Police Department's secret intelligence unit, Lt. Earl Kynette, had planned and carried out a car bombing against a former police officer who was investigating corruption in city hall. Although surgeons removed over 150 pieces of shrapnel from the victim, Harry Raymond, he miraculously survived. Raymond's subsequent court testimony proved instrumental in removing the administration of Mayor Frank Shaw for complicity in the affair.[44]

While Shaw had successfully run for mayor in 1933 on a platform of "honesty in government," his administration proved to be one of the most corrupt in American history. Under the Shaw administration, gambling and prostitution were openly tolerated as long as bribes and pay-offs were made to City Hall. The corruption also reached into the Los Angeles Police Department where positions of rank were bought and sold. The eventual conviction of Lt. Kynette for the attempted murder of Harry Raymond, and the conviction of Joe Shaw, the mayor's brother, on 66 counts of corruption led to the defeat of Mayor Shaw in a special recall election. Shaw's reversal at the polls accorded him the dubious distinction of being the first mayor of a major American city to be publicly recalled.[45]

The man who defeated Shaw at the polls was Fletcher Bowron, a shy, rather stodgy former Superior Court judge. Bowron's subdued physical appearance and judge-like demeanor signalled to the electorate that serious reforms would take place. Upon taking office, Bowron began his tenure with a thorough house cleaning. In the L.A.P.D. alone, Bowron had nearly 500 police officers fired, demoted, or transferred. To the public at large, Bowron frequently stated his goals of eradicating political corruption and the establishment of a professional municipal government. While

Bowron's success at ending local political corruption is subject to debate, his ability to manage municipal government is considered by many observers to have been exemplary.

The Los Angeles Bowron inherited was a colorful one. Hollywood was at its zenith. In 1939, American movie-goers were buying tickets at a rate of 80 million a week. To meet the frantic demand for its product, Hollywood studios were literally producing a movie a day. Despite the hectic pace, some of Hollywood's greatest classics were made, including, *Gone With the Wind*, *The Wizard of Oz*, *Stagecoach*, and *Young Mr. Lincoln*. 1939 also marked the first screen appearances of such future movie legends as John Wayne, Bob Hope, Jimmy Stewart, Judy Garland, Henry Fonda, Laurence Olivier, and Ingrid Bergman.[46] The 365 movies produced in 1939 earned Hollywood more than $700 million. The earning power of Hollywood thus made the movies the nation's 11th largest industry.[47]

While Hollywood often depicted prewar Los Angeles as a center of wealth and high living, writers living there often focused their works on the city's dark underside. Prominent among them was Raymond Chandler, a local oil industry accountant turned writer. Among the classics that bear his authorship are the two prewar mystery novels, *The Big Sleep* (1939) and *Farewell, My Lovely* (1940). In both novels, Chandler's protagonist, the private detective Philip Marlowe, finds the people of Los Angeles to be as deceptive as the city's tranquil appearance. Although Chandler's works were fictional, his books helped to temper the American public's image of Los Angeles as the "City of Angels."[48]

Like Chandler, novelist Nathanael West was not taken in by the city's swaying palm trees and calm blue skies. West also wrote of the city's many seedy characters and its seamy underside. His 1939 novel, *Day of the Locust*, focuses on the shattered dreams of those who sought "fame and fortune" in the illusionary world of Hollywood.

Despite such warnings, thousands continued to migrate to Los Angeles. In truth, Los Angeles was a place where one could leave their past behind and start anew. Further, Los Angeles seemed fresh and vibrant, especially when compared to the small rural towns that many had left behind.

As thousands continued to pour into the Southland, both the local and federal government struggled to meet the region's pressing needs. Two historic obstacles continually hindered the city's development: the scarcity of fresh water, and the region's continued isolation from the more industrialized East. In 1939, two public works projects came to fruition, offering

Thousands turn out for the opening of Union Station in May 1939. The new station helps to link Los Angeles with the rest of the nation. (Photograph courtesy of the University of Southern California's Regional History Center.)

both hope and partial solution to these age-old problems. In early May, the Union Railway Station was opened amid large civic celebration. The station, named Union for the unity of three railroad lines—the Santa Fe, Union Pacific and Southern Pacific, quickly established itself as the central transit point for rapid railroad service between the West and eastern sections of the country. Just six months later, desperately needed water began to make its way into Southern California through the Colorado River Aqueduct. Ironically, city leaders in 1939 had worried that Los Angeles would now have too much water for its needs.

These two predominantly federally financed developments were completed just in time. By early 1940, defense orders from around the world began pouring into the Southland, and Los Angeles seemed to expand with each order. Blessed with large territorial size, a rapidly growing population, and a strong adaptable industrial base, the region emerged expectantly out of the Great Depression. Although increased demand for war production spelled prosperity, its portent caused concern. In May 1940, faced with the more likely prospect of American involvement in a world war, Mayor Bowron began organizing what became known as the "Defense Committee of Southern California."

The Defense Committee, which consisted of over two hundred local civic leaders, particularly from the fields of business and industry, sought to coordinate their activities in the hopes of strengthening Los Angeles' defense. In consultation with the War Department, Navy Department, and a host of state and federal agencies, the Committee developed intricate plans to protect the region from attack. Subcommittees were also formed to maintain the area's vital defense production in the event of American intervention in Europe, Asia or both. Interestingly, each subcommittee was either headed or staffed by a department manager of the Los Angeles Chamber of Commerce.[49] The link between defense production and the region's economic health was not lost on local civic leaders. As the Defense Committee continued its work, another delegation from the Los Angeles Chamber of Commerce went to Washington D.C. and opened an information office in the hopes of obtaining more government contracts for the Southland.[50]

Mayor Bowron, center, inspects a section of the new Colorado River Aqueduct. In the background is the Coxcomb tunnel, one of the 38 hard rock tunnels dug for the aqueduct system. (Photograph courtesy of the University of Southern California's Regional History Center.)

The fleet at peaceful anchor in September 1938. As tensions with Japan increase, the fleet is moved from San Pedro to Pearl Harbor, Hawaii, in May 1940. (Photograph courtesy of the United States Naval Institute.)

As war approached, the pace of Los Angeles' industrial conversion quickened. Most plants, to the delight of the unemployed, increased their hiring and added swing shifts. The companies also bought large tracts of farm land upon which they quickly built additional factories. As the rapid industrial expansion continued, word came that the Los Angeles-based Pacific Fleet had been ordered by President Roosevelt to move to Pearl Harbor, Hawaii, as part of America's forward defense against continued Japanese expansionism.

In May 1940, as crowds of friends and family watched from the docks, anchors were weighed and the mighty battleships of the Pacific fleet slowly sailed towards the distant horizon. While some of the sailors aboard the ships excitedly spoke of the move to the "island paradise," others gazed a quiet and reluctant farewell to the city they called home. None aboard the ships, though, imagined that this was the fleet's final farewell to Los Angeles. None, too, anticipated the "day of infamy" that awaited them on a December Sunday morning a year and a half later.

Endnotes

1. Los Angeles *Times,* October 27, 1991.
2. The city's first freeway was the six mile Arroyo Seco Parkway which was opened on December 30, 1940. The Parkway was later renamed the Pasadena Freeway upon the addition of a 2.2 mile four level interchange in 1953. For additional information see, Los Angeles *Times,* December 21, 1991.
3. Willard F. Motley, "Small Town Los Angeles," *Commonweal,* 30 (June 30, 1939), pp. 251-252.
4. Phillip Neff, Lisette C. Baum, and Grace E. Heilman, *Favored Industries in Los Anqeles: An Analysis of Production Costs* (Los Angeles: The Haynes Foundation, 1948), p. 7.
5. John Parke Young, "Industrial Background," in George W. Robbins and L. Deming Tilton, eds., *Preface to a Master Plan* (Los Angeles: The Pacific Southwest Academy, 1941), p. 61.
6. Los Angeles County Chamber of Commerce, Industrial Department, "Economic Background of Los Angeles County," *in Collection of Eight Studies on the Industrial Development of Los Angeles County* (Los Angeles Chamber of Commerce, n.d.), p. 6.
7. Los Angeles *Times,* January 4, 1939.
8. Leonard Leader, "Los Angeles and the Great Depression," (Ph.D. dissertation, University of California, Los Angeles, 1972), pp. 266-269.
9. John Parke Young, "Industrial Background," in Robbins and Tilton, eds., *Preface to a Master Plan,* pp. 69-72.
10. Geoffrey Perrett, *Days of Sadness, Years of Triumph: The American People, 1939-1945* (New York: Coward, McCann and Geoghegan Inc., 1973), p. 29.
11. Phillip Neff, Lisette C. Baum, and Grace E. Heilman, *Favored Industries in Los Angeles: An Analysis of Production Costs* (Los Angeles, 1948), p. 7. Phillip Neff and Annette Weifenbach, *Business Cycles in Selected Industrial Areas* (Berkeley and Los Angeles, 1949), pp. 165-194.
12. Los Angeles Chamber of Commerce, "Economic Background of Los Angeles County," p. 6.

13. Wayne Biddie, *Barons of the Sky: From Early Flight to Strategic Warfare. The Story of the American Aerospace Industry* (New York: Simon and Schuster, 1991), p. 123.
14. James Richard Wilburn, "Social and Economic Aspects of the Aircraft Industry in Metropolitan Los Angeles During World War II," (Ph.D. dissertation, University of California, Los Angeles, 1971), p. 32.
15. Ibid., pp. 32-34.
16. Ibid., pp. 30-34.
17. Coons and Miller, *Economic and Industrial Survey,* p. 184.
18. Ibid., p. 198.
19. Ibid., p. 125.
20. Carey McWilliams, *Southern California Country: An Island on the Land* (New York: Duell, Sloan & Pearce, 1946), p. 233.
21. Clifford M. Zierer, "The Land Use Patterns," in Robbins and Tilton, eds., *A Preface to a Master Plan,* pp. 46-55.
22. Jacqueline Rorabeck Kasun, *Some Social Aspects of Business Cycles in the Los Angeles Area, 1920-1950* (Los Angeles: The Haynes Foundation, n.d.), p. 10.
23. Constantine Panunzio, "Growth and Character of the Population," in Robbins and Tilton, eds., *A Preface to a Master Plan,* p. 30.
24. Kasun, *Some Social Aspects,* p. 13.
25. Earl Hanson, *Los Angeles County Population and Housing Data: Statistical Data from the 1940 Census* (Los Angeles: The Haynes Foundation, 1944), p. 14.
26. Commonwealth Club of California, *The Population of California* (San Francisco: California Research Service, 1946), p. 127.
27. Kasun, *Some Social Aspects,* pp. 24-33.
28. Scott Bottles, "The Making of the Modern City: Los Angeles and the Automobile, 1900-1950," (Ph.D. dissertation, University of California, Los Angeles, 1984), p. 14.
29. Andrew F. Rolle, *Los Angeles: From Pueblo to* City, (San Francisco: Boyd and Fraser Press, 1981), p. 50.

30. Ed Ainsworth, *Out of the Noose! Way Pointed for American Cities to Save Themselves from Traffic Stagnation* (Los Angeles: Automobile Club of Southern California, 1938), p. 30.

31. E.E. East, "Streets: The Circulatory System," in Robbins and Tilton, eds., *A Preface to a Master Plan,* p. 94.

32. Transportation Engineering Board, City of Los Angeles, *Report of Traffic and Transportation Survey* (Los Angeles: Citizen's Transportation Survey Committee, 1940), pp. 14-27.

33. Ainsworth, *Out of the Noose!,* p. 30.

34. Los Angeles *Times,* December 21, 1990.

35. Bottles, "The Making of the Modern City," p. 296.

36. For an excellent overview of the early development of the oil industry in Los Angeles see Fred W. Viehe, "Black Gold Suburbs: The Influence of the Extractive Industry on the Suburbanization of Los Angeles, 1890-1930," *Journal of Urban History* (November 1981), pp. 1-26.

37. Security-First National Bank of Los Angeles, *Monthly Summary of Business Conditions in Southern California,* August 1941.

38. Ibid.

39. Harvey M. Beigel, *Battleship Country: The Battle Fleet at San Pedro-Long Beach, California - 1919-1940* (Missoula, Montana: Pictorial Histories Publishing Co., 1983) p.1.

40. Ibid., p. 71.

41. Robert Smith Thompson, *A Time for War: Franklin D. Roosevelt and the Path to Pearl Harbor* (New York: Prentice-Hall, 1991), pp. 176-179.

42. Cornero's contention that the gambling ships were operating in international waters and therefore immune to persecution was not untenable. His case was fought all the way to the California Supreme Court who ruled against him in *People v. Stralla,* 14 Cal. 2d. 1939, p. 633.

43. For more detailed accounts of the colorful legacy of Tony Cornero's *Rex,* Bruce Henstell, *Sunshine and Wealth: Los Angeles in the Twenties and Thirties* (San Francisco: Chronicle Books, 1984), pp. 64-71.; and 'Admiral' Tony Cornero and the Battle of Santa Monica Bay" in Marvin J. Wolfe and Katherine Mader's, *Fallen Angels: Chronicles of L.A. Crime and Mystery* (New York: Ballantine Books, 1986), pp. 179-186.

44. Wolf and Mader, *Fallen Angels,* pp. 171-176.

45. Fred W. Viehe, "The Recall of Mayor Frank L. Shaw: A Revision," *California History,* 59:4 (1980-81), p. 290-305.

46. Los Angeles *Times,* July 22, 1991.

47. Ibid., January 1, 1989.

48. Chandler himself grew tired of the city and moved to the beach community of La Jolla in 1946.

49. *Handbook of Information: Prepared for the Defense Committee of Southern California.* Anson Ford Manuscripts, Box 66, Henry L. Huntington Library, San Marino, California. Ford was a member of the Los Angeles County Board of Supervisors between 1934-1958. He was also instrumental in aiding Fletcher Bowron's successful election as mayor in 1938.

50. Gerald D. Nash, *The American West Transformed: The Impact of the Second World War* (Bloomington: Indiana University Press, 1985), pp. 7-8.

The Defense of Los Angeles

2

The surprise Japanese attack at Pearl Harbor, while a shock to all Americans, hit Los Angeles particularly hard. Given Los Angeles' deep ties to the Pacific Fleet and its sailors, a shared sense of grief swept through the city as news of the naval force's near destruction made its way back to the mainland. Grief, however, soon gave way to fear and anger. Much of the local anger was directed against the resident Japanese-American community. Despite their protestations of loyalty to the United States, many Japanese community leaders were quickly "rounded-up" in police and F.B.I. raids during the afternoon and evening of December 7, 1941.

Suspicion and prejudice against the Japanese-American community had been a long-standing condition in Los Angeles. Despite their exemplary record as loyal American citizens, Japanese-Americans were often

A far cry from the days in L.A. The U.S.S. *Arizona* afire amidst the Japanese attack on Pearl Harbor, December 7, 1941. The death toll abroad the *Arizona* was the highest of any single warship in United States naval history. (Photograph courtesy of National Archives)

relegated to working in Southern California as fishermen, gardeners and farmers. The attack on Pearl Harbor only exacerbated these prejudices as many Angelenos lumped together the interests of local Japanese-Americans with those of the enemy nation of Japan. Many in Los Angeles also held the mistaken belief that Japan would quickly fall to American military might. One optimistic young man, interviewed the day after the attack on Pearl Harbor, stated, "I think Japan has made a mistake. How can she withstand any attack by our great forces!" Echoing that confidence was the belief that the war would be short. "We should be able to clean up on those fellows in six weeks or less," claimed another Los Angeles *Times* interviewee.[1] But in truth, the American military was hardly prepared to fight the two-front war that it was now entering. In several American boot camps military inductees were actually practicing with broom sticks against paper mache tanks.[2] And out in the Pacific the American military continued to take heavy losses against Japanese aggression. So grim was the situation in the early days of the war that the War Department withheld photos and damage assessments of the attack at Pearl Harbor for fear of inciting panic in the American citizenry.

As the shock of Pearl Harbor slowly subsided, fear began to sweep through the Los Angeles basin. Many citizens worried that the city itself would soon be the target of a Japanese military attack. Several local newspapers exacerbated these fears by pointing out that the Hawaiian islands were only 2,550 miles away from California. In truth, the surface fleet of the Japanese Navy had been stretched to the limits in carrying out the attack on Pearl Harbor. Still, this was unknown to the public. Comedic actor and writer Buck Henry humorously recalls the city's then trepidation, "We imagined parachutes dropping. We imagined the hills of Hollywood on fire. We imagined hand-to-hand combat on Rodeo Drive."[3]

The city's apprehension is understandable given that by 1939, Los Angeles had become the key industrial production center of the western United States. Further, it was home to the "Big Six" aircraft plants—Douglas, Lockheed, North American, Northrop, Vega, and Vultee. Thus, with the outbreak of hostilities with Japan, Los Angeles had become the vital defense link for American military operations in the Pacific.

Given Los Angeles' strategic value, there was great concern for its security. Confronting a daunting task both civic and military leaders met to plan the region's defense. Encompassing 451 square miles, Los Angeles was larger in area than Chicago, San Francisco, Philadelphia and Seattle combined.[4] Further, the region's irregular pattern of development created confusing entanglements of jurisdictions that hindered the response time

Paradise Lost. Stunned sailors watch in disbelief as Japanese aircraft destroy a naval airfield at Pearl Harbor. (Photograph courtesy of the National Archives)

of proper authorities in emergencies. Fortunately for the Los Angeles County region, a workable emergency response plan was already in place prior to December 7, 1941. This groundwork stemmed from the region's experiences with natural disasters such as fires, floods, and earthquakes.

Using past local disaster plans as guides, civil defense organizers formulated a comprehensive plan that would allow each of the forty-five cities of Los Angeles County to retain local control for their own civil defense programs, while at the same time coordinating those efforts to meet the region's defense needs.[5]

Civil defense planners in Los Angeles received a scare on Christmas Eve, 1941, when the American lumber carrier SS *Absaroka* was torpedoed by a Japanese submarine in the Catalina Channel. The attack, which was witnessed by onlookers from White Point in San Pedro, killed one crewman, but failed to sink the ship. To the cheers of the hillside spectators, the ship limped back into the Los Angeles harbor despite a large gaping hole in its port side.[6]

A newsboy on the afternoon of December 7, 1941 in Los Angeles' Little Tokyo district. (Photograph courtesy of the University of Southern California's Regional History Center).

This off-shore attack proved the vulnerability of maritime shipping along the west coast.[7] The coast's usual protector, the United States Pacific Fleet, was now busily attempting a forward defense of the Pacific. With the mainstay of the Pacific Fleet thousands of miles away, approximately twelve Japanese submarines began attacking American shipping along the coast from Seattle to San Diego. West coast military leaders and civil defense planners feared that the menacing submarines were the front line of an eventual Japanese carrier force whose planes could launch a devastating attack on the American mainland. These defense officials feared Los Angeles would prove a tempting target, given the region's vital aircraft plants, shipyards, refineries, and military installations.[8]

In response to these understandable fears, military authorities in Washington quickly rushed troops and supplies to the west coast. As armed soldiers and Coast Guard personnel patrolled the beaches, bunkers with machine guns and artillery pieces were strategically placed along the city's coastline. To protect Los Angeles from an air attack, large barrage balloons were anchored over the city, their steel cables specifically designed to entangle low-flying enemy aircraft. Often well hidden and thought to be the most effective deterrent against air attack were large antiaircraft guns that were placed throughout the city.

To further guard against an air attack, civil defense officials instituted nightly blackouts, which began on the evening of December 10, 1941. Unfortunately for the civil defense authorities, the first night under blackout proved immensely confusing for many in Los Angeles. Although more than 8,000 air-raid wardens made it to their posts, and thousands of street lights were successfully turned off by public service workers, many Angelenos were unprepared for the ensuing darkness. In the city's downtown, numerous workers suddenly found themselves stranded in darkened office buildings. Others in their vehicles at the time of the blackout continued to drive but in the spirit of the blackout, did so without turning on their headlights. Numerous car accidents resulted. Consequently, the emergency room at the city's Central Hospital quickly filled beyond capacity. Doctors there, operating by lanterns, handled eighty-six major injuries in the first four hours of the blackout.[9]

As this December 11, 1941 night photo shows, Los Angeles had a lot to learn about proper blackout procedures. Before long, however, the city made commendable adjustments to life under blackouts. (Photograph courtesy of the University of Southern California's Regional History Center).

Appearing from the air as a verdant farm field is the well camouflaged Douglas Aircraft plant in El Segundo. (Photograph courtesy of the National Archives)

Los Angeles' first experience with a blackout did, however, prove effective in pointing out the need for an "at war" mentality by the city's civilian population. Residents who had displayed their Christmas lights prior to the night of December 10, now unhesitatingly took them down. And civil defense officials reevaluated their previous demand that all defense-related plants cease operations during nightly blackouts. The defense planners realized the city's war plants were just too important to the Allied war effort to be shut down even when a general blackout was in effect.

As painters painted over defense plant windows, military authorities began to make extra efforts to further protect the plants from Japanese air attacks. Besides placing antiaircraft emplacements around the factories, Hollywood set designers were brought in to camouflage the large manufacturing operations. Within weeks, several aircraft assembly plants appeared from the air to be verdant hills and quiet city streets.[10]

As the city fortified itself against a possible Japanese attack, questions were raised in the media about the true loyalties of the Japanese-American community.

The respected Los Angeles *Times*, whose lead articles on the day following the attack on Pearl Harbor had assured readers that many local Japanese-Americans were "loyal Americans," abruptly reversed its posture and began playing up stories of Asian disloyalty. Such headlines as, "Asiatic, Who Had Pledged Loyalty, Found with Guns," played well to growing public paranoia and resentment towards the Japanese-American community.

Local politicians at first seemed ambivalent as to what to do with the Japanese-American community. In the days following Pearl Harbor, politicians and other civic leaders channeled the citizenry's anger into constructive behavior. Residents within the city of Los Angeles were asked to join and participate in the city's Citizen's Defense Corps. Started in May 1941, membership in the Defense Corps grew rapidly. Within nine months

A round-up of 'suspects' in Los Angeles on the evening of December 7, 1941. In contrast to the Japanese community of Hawaii, Japanese and Japanese-Americans in Los Angeles would be forcibly interned in relocation camps beginning in February, 1942. (Photograph courtesy of the University of Southern California's Regional History Center).

of the Japanese attack on Pearl Harbor, more than 165,000 volunteers, nearly one in ten of the city's residents, had become active members of the program. Trained by the city's police and fire departments, volunteers took positions as air raid wardens, fire reporters, messengers and auxiliary police officers.[11]

Although the city's civil defense program faced severe budget constraints, members of the civilian defense corps used ingenuity to secure much needed equipment. Milk and ice delivery companies, whose operations were restricted by federal regulations, were contacted for the use of their second-hand trucks. Seventy-three working trucks, outfitted with old but still usable hoses, axes, and shovels were soon in use by auxiliary firefighters. Firefighting brigades, not fortunate to obtain a second-hand truck, often constructed their own equipment by using children's wagons, discarded water heaters and gasoline motors from lawn mowers.

The shortage of government funding forced auxiliary firefighters and air raid wardens to raise their own revenues to pay for such equipment as phones, shelter, and postage. Money for these services was raised through such activities as dances, picnics, card parties, and even prize fights. Given the dramatic population growth of Los Angeles during the war years, these fund-raising efforts had the salutary effect of bringing the city's residents together.[12] In conjunction with the Citizen's Defense Corps, the Los Angeles City Defense Council was also formed in May 1941. The Defense Council, composed of the mayor, two city officials, and twelve leading citizens, acted as an advisory board for the city's civil defense. Among the council's key contributions was the establishment of the Consumer Information Center whose volunteers aided consumers through the labyrinth of war-imposed restrictions. The Center also provided educational programs on how to make the best use of food items, clothing materials, and other essential items that were restricted by the war effort.[13]

The Defense Council also successfully lobbied for the adoption of staggered work schedules throughout the city in order to reduce the growing traffic congestion that threatened war production. The Council also tackled problems of health and nutrition, rent control, and citizen morale.

Challenged to meet the needs brought about by all-out war, departments within the Los Angeles city bureaucracy found themselves doing more with less money. The city's playground and recreational department, for example, began turning public playgrounds into physical fitness centers for future draftees. The department also expanded the scope of its operations to supervise thousands of children whose parents were working long hours aiding the war effort. The city's Public Works Department found itself busy dimming street lights each evening, and was also responsible for securing rights-of-way for defense transportation.[14] And the city's retirement system office struggled to keep city employees on the job fearing that large numbers of municipal workers would be enticed away to higher paying defense jobs.

Although the city government remained strapped for funds during the war, it nonetheless succeeded in organizing a functioning civil defense system that became a model for other communities in the United States. At the heart of the city's civil defense system were twelve district control centers which were dispersed throughout the city according to population density and the location of strategic industries. Operating 24 hours a day and staffed by police, fire, public works and Red Cross personnel, each control center was set to respond to any public emergency. Coordinating the district control center's operations was a large central control center run by full-time city employees. All of the centers, though, particularly benefited from the volunteer work of hundreds of citizens who served as radio and telephone operators, messengers, and recording clerks.[15]

Each of the control centers was linked to air raid warden zones whose precincts were responsible for the protection on average of 547 persons. A precursor to today's 911 emergency phone response system, the control centers carefully recorded each call received and then gave that information to the emergency service responsible for responding. All of the control center personnel, which numbered more than three thousand, were trained to advise citizens on matters of first aid, gas warfare defense, and incendiary firefighting.[16]

While the threat of a possible hostile attack brought forth a spirit of civic participation, problems arose in regard to the inclusion of women in the civil defense effort. Civil defense planners, although in desperate need of workers, encouraged women to volunteer for civil defense responsibilities considered "appropriate" for their sex. Thus, the local media carried appeals for women to volunteer as nurses, typists, and telephone receptionists. Unfortunately, many were unable to because they were already too busy working in defense plants. Hence the ironic appeal of Mrs. Stearns Thayer, president of the California Federation of Women's Clubs, who pleaded for female volunteers to work in nursery schools because "in the area of defense industries women are taking jobs and the children are becoming a problem of the whole community."[17]

Many women's groups sought to change the public's perception of their capabilities by demonstrating their effectiveness in local civil defense work. Under the Los Angeles *Times* headline "Beverly Hills Women Proving They'd Like Tough War Jobs," an article stated that each of the city's 400-member Women's Emergency Corps were capable of driving an ambulance, riding a horse, rendering first aid, doing minor vehicle repair work, and shooting rifles and pistols.[18] Still, civil defense work in the early days of the war was considered "a man's job." In the city of Los Angeles, women air-raid wardens were only allowed to serve during daylight hours. And the city's auxiliary police force faced a continual shortage of women volunteers. When queried about the shortage of female volunteers, a police representative stated that it stemmed, "from a general lack of understanding of the important responsibility traffic policewomen will have under emergency conditions." In truth, the lack of understanding might have come from the fact that although women received the same arduous training as male auxiliary police personnel, they were not allowed to ride

An example Los Angeles' around-the-clock plane production is this squadron of P-51 Mustangs that are parked at Los Angeles in 1943. At the far right is camouflage netting that was used to conceal the airport's activities. (Photograph courtesy of the Los Angeles Department of Airports).

in patrol cars or walk police beats. Women auxiliary police officers were assigned only to traffic control duty and only during daylight hours.[19]

Regardless of the prewar roles of women, and the initial difficulties of attracting them into some postions previously reserved for men, the demands of the war brought large-scale changes for women. As one War Department official informed a gathering of Southern California defense officials, "Women are as capable and productive as men and they must be so used. Prejudice, convenience and inertia can no longer bar their full employment."[20] As the ranks of local men continued to be depleted by the war effort, women assumed a greater role in civil defense and in war production. This newly discovered appreciation of women's abilities allowed civil defense authorities to expand their operations, thus enhancing the area's security. Furthermore, the employment of local women in war production reduced the need for the recruitment of outside workers, which in turn helped ease the burden on government authorities in the areas of civil defense, housing, transportation, and sanitation.[21]

The successful integration of women into the region's civil defense effort also promoted the involvement of retired persons as well as young school boys. Using retired persons often brought needed leadership and experience vital to the volunteer organizations. Further, retired workers were able to devote energy and time to civil defense groups which school age children could not.

Young males aged 15–21 readily found work in the messenger and fire watching services. Those participating as messengers were required to complete forty-four hours of training. In the event of a disabling attack, or if for any reason a communication failure developed, these young men were responsible for handling important communications for civil defense authorities. Like their fire watcher counterparts, the voluntary participation of the area's male youth enabled many of them to acquire a sense of civic duty and responsibility.[22] As civil defense officials relied more and more on groups of women, retired persons and young men, they increasingly found themselves in competition with industry for these previously overlooked segments of the population.

While unemployment in Los Angeles in 1940 reached a staggering 13 percent, the problem evaporated in 1941 as unskilled positions became available in both the aircraft and ship building industries.[23] Yet despite these new high paying job opportunities, thousands remained committed to the region's civil defense. Auxiliary firefighters, for example, provided necessary support to the city's fire department, which by November 1943, had 362 vacancies, while at the same time experiencing an increase in emergency calls from 16,092 in 1941, to more than 20,000 in 1943.[24]

As civil defense efforts kicked into high gear, the public grew more fearful of a Japanese air attack. Mayor Bowron sought to reassure Los Angeles residents by declaring that he and other defense council officials did not "expect a bombing locally."[25] Yet the public's fear seemed to grow as local news stories continued to hint that the Japanese-American community was in alliance with the Japanese war machine. One Los Angeles *Times* story printed on February 23, 1942, told of weekend raids that succeeded in the breaking up of "secret societies organized as espionage centers" and the capture of "scores of alien reserve officers, particularly Japanese." The raids, described as "the first triumphs of the war in the Pacific Coast states" were alleged to have "ended the careers of many saboteurs before they began."

Unfortunately for the Japanese-American community, a Japanese submarine shelled the oil storage area of Ellwood, 12 miles north of Santa Barbara only hours after the article appeared. Although the attack inflicted little damage, it substantially heightened fears that Los Angeles itself could easily be attacked.[26] Lampooning any remaining doubters, the Los Angeles *Times* ran an editorial cartoon showing a complacent citizen being shelled from offshore with the words, "It could happen here" written in the projectile's trail.[27]

On February 25, two nights after the Japanese submarine's shelling of Ellwood's oil storage area, army officials warned Los Angeles civil defense authorities that enemy aircraft were seen approaching the Los Angeles area. At 2:25 a.m. the region's defenses went into full alert, with antiaircraft guns firing into searchlight-swept skies. Many witnesses to the event believe that the authorities mistook a wayward weather balloon for a Japanese plane. Although the raid's authenticity became a source of debate among military officials, no bombs were dropped and no planes were shot down.[28] However, the event known today as the "Battle of Los Angeles," gave the city's residents a genuine feeling of being at war. It also gave "locals" a story that is still recounted as a now fond wartime memory. Comedian Bob Hope recalled that during the "attack," two air raid wardens in Beverly Hills, the Austrian born movie director Otto Preminger and German-born producer Henry Blake, ran up and down Rexford Drive screaming, "Close de vindows! Close de vindows!" In response, a frightened movie star ran out of his front door yelling, "Run for your lives! The Germans are here!"[29] Although the only shells that actually fell on Los Angeles that night were from the city's own anti-

Especially popular with visiting troops was a night at Ken Murray's somewhat risque "Blackout Shows." (Photograph courtesy of the University of Southern California's Regional History Center).

aircraft guns, local residents felt that they were beginning to experience the full impact of the war. City streets were quickly becoming crowded with sailors, marines, and soldiers. Many of the young sailors and marines, destined to fight and die in the Pacific theatre, had their orders given to them at the large Naval and Marine Corps Armory which had recently been built adjacent to the city's downtown. Completed in 1940, the Los Angeles armory was the largest facility for reservists in the United States. Virtually everyone who joined the navy from the West coast during the war passed through its doors.[30]

Growing numbers of troops also began pouring into the confines of the city's Ft. MacArthur. Originally designed in 1914 to protect Los Angeles Harbor, the fort in the anxiety filled days following Pearl Harbor, sought to ease citizen fears of Japanese attack by promoting itself as the "Guardian of Los Angeles." In truth, its powerful 16-inch and 14-inch guns were virtually useless against an air attack over the city. Nonetheless, while many coastal windows were shattered as the big guns were tested, the loud explosions seemed to reassure Angelenos throughout the city that American military might was as close as the city's shoreline.[31]

In other ways, too, residents began to feel and sense the effects of the war. In early 1942, the federal government began releasing a long list of consumer goods banned from production. Metal, for example, which was desperately needed for building planes, ships, and tanks, forced the discontinuance of the production of new cars, washing machines, refrigerators, and even metal coat hangers. Particularly galling to some women was the ban on nylon. Needed for parachutes, what little nylon was available often became the source of black market activity or of actual theft from parachute factory floors. While some women complained of the loss of their nylon stockings, many youngsters rejoiced that dreaded Castor oil was off store shelves.

In May, 1942, full-scale rationing was begun through the federal government's Office of Price Administration (OPA). Under the OPA's direction, the War and Price Rationing Program began issuing 131 million

Mayor Bowron receives pots and pans gathered from an aluminum scrap drive. (Photograph courtesy of the University of Southern California's Regional History Center).

war rationing books. The effects were almost immediate. Traffic congestion quickly decreased as consumers faced sharp restrictions on their gasoline usage.

Many residents found themselves with growing savings but little opportunity to spend it on consumer goods. One popular and available avenue was entertainment. Long-time residents and new arrivals alike crowded into theatres to enjoy Ken Murray's vaudeville-like show, "Blackouts of 1942." The show, at the downtown El Capitan, was headlined by a young newcomer named Desi Arnaz. Especially popular with defense workers were evening "swing shift" dances held on various beach piers. Police in Santa Monica, however, sought a discontinuance of the 12:30 to 6:00 A.M. dances, after repeated confrontations with large, disorderly crowds.[32] Incensed that some revelers were not taking the war seriously enough, Los Angeles Chamber of Commerce President Carleton Tibbets stated, "For a nation supposedly fighting a losing battle against vicious and deadly foes, most of our people are having a pretty good time of it!"[33]

One entertainment business victim of wartime rationing was Gay's Lion Farm in El Monte. The five-acre site, home to 217 lions, including "Leo," the snarling and roaring symbol of Hollywood's then most powerful studio, Metro-Goldwyn-Mayer, had opened in 1925. Owned and operated by husband and wife, Charles and Muriel Gay, the Lion Farm trained lions for zoos, circuses and the movie industry. It was also a popular tourist attraction, having drawn over a million visitors, including Eleanor Roosevelt and Albert Einstein. The Lion Farm was especially popular with local residents who enjoyed hearing the "Lion Glee Club," which took place on Monday nights, the only night of the week when the lions were not fed. Although the lions had been responsible for the deaths of two trainers, the Lion Farm was financially successful until wartime rationing. The implementation of gasoline rationing quickly cut tourist revenues, and the lions themselves were forced to suffer through wartime meat rationing. By December 1942, the Gay's reluctantly decided to close the park, thus ending a colorful chapter in Los Angeles tourist attraction history.[34] As residents became more acclimatized to wartime restrictions, a sense of ingenuity seemed to take hold throughout the city. Many housewives became proficient at getting the most out of rationed food products, proudly boasting that nothing was ever wasted. In fact, homemakers played an integral defense role by saving kitchen fat that would later be used to produce glycerine, an important component of gunpowder. Others, however, used ingenious methods to circumvent gas and tire rationing. Black market activities such as bartering and pay-offs were commonplace. Still, a sense of humor was maintained about the cumbersome government restrictions. When told he could not inform his baseball listeners about the weather conditions at the ballgame he was announcing for fear that information could assist enemy attackers, the ever colorful Dizzy Dean got around the problem by stating, "I ain't saying nothin' about the weather, but I'd advise you women listenin' to get your washes off the closeline."

Most Angelenos readily accepted the growing government restrictions, especially in light of continual dark news emanating from both the European and Pacific war fronts. Given that the Pacific war was geographically closer to Los Angeles accounts of the disaster at Pearl Harbor, followed shortly by the announcement of the fall of Bataan to the Japanese in early April, 1942, dampened any American hopes of a quick victory in the Pacific. Local residents, imitating their counterparts in London, England remained stoic and steeled themselves for a long, arduous war. And despite continual news of American setbacks in the early days of the war, many in Los Angeles remained optimistic that the Allied forces would ultimately prevail.

From the otherwise gloommy news of Pacific setbacks, a ray of hope emerged with the surprising announcement that Japan had been bombed by sixteen American B-25 Mitchell bombers on April 18, 1942. The daring raid, launched from the deck of the U.S. Aircraft Carrier *Hornet*, marked the first time in history that Japan had been attacked by air. Although the bombing raid inflicted little damage, it served to dramatically raise the nation's morale. While much of the United States rejoiced at the news of the air attack, Los Angeles newspapers noted with beaming pride that the raid's leader, Lt. Col. James "Jimmie" Doolittle, had locally attended Manual Arts High School, and had graduated from Los Angeles Junior College in 1916.

Beyond boosting civic pride, the "Doolittle Raid" calmed fears of a Japanese attack on Los Angeles. The city's previous energies, which had been defensive in nature, now became oriented towards bringing the war to the enemy. Thus, with a renewed sense of fighting spirit, many local manufacturers quickly expanded their factory floor space and added still more workers to their payrolls. Other factories, not previously on a twenty-four hour production schedule, began around-the-clock operations. Out of this massive industrial expansion and popular fighting spirit, Los Angeles rapidly became the world's airborne arsenal of democracy.

Endnotes

1. Los Angeles *Times,* December 8, 1941.
2. Ross Gregory, *America 1941: A Nation at the Crossroads,* (New York: The Free Press, 1989), p. 34.
3. Los Angeles *Times,* September 1, 1992.
4. "Civilian Defense in Los Angeles," *Western City 18,* (September, 1942), p. 20.
5. Los Angeles *Times,* December 8, 1941.
6. *The Daily Breeze,* February 23, 1992.
7. On December 23, 1941 Japanese submarines sank the Los Angeles-based Union Oil Tanker *Montebello* off the California central coast. Much like the *Absaroka* crowds of onlookers on-shore witnessed the attack. Fortunately, all hands survived. Los Angeles *Times,* December 24, 1941.
8. Ibid.
9. "Your City Geared to Defense," Los Angeles *Year Book 1941,* (City of Los Angeles, 1941), p. 27.
10. James Richard Wilburn, "Social and Economic Aspects of the Aircraft in Metropolitan Los Angeles During World War II," (Ph.D. dissertation, University of California, Los Angeles, 1971), p. 43.
11. "Civilian Defense in Los Angeles," p. 30.
12. Ibid., pp. 26–31.
13. "Your City Geared to Defense," p. 10.
14. Ibid., pp. 38–41.
15. "Civilian Defense in Los Angeles," pp. 22–24.
16. Ibid., pp. 22–24.
17. Los Angeles *Times,* December 11, 1941.
18. Ibid., December 14, 1941.
19. "Civilian Defense in Los Angeles," p. 32.
20. Los Angeles *Times,* December 11, 1941.

21. 78th Congress, First Sess., House, Subcommittee of Committee on Naval Affairs, *Hearings on Congested* Areas, part 8, p. 1973. (8 parts, Washington, *1944),* hereafter cited as *Congested Area Hearings.*

22. "Civilian Defense in Los Angeles," p. 33.

23. United States Bureau of the Census, "Characteristics of the Population, Labor Force, Families, and Housing, Los Angeles Congested Production Area: April, 1944," Series CA–3, #5, p. 1.

24. Los Angeles *Year Book 1941,* p. 25; *Congested Area Hearings,* p. 1999.

25. Los Angeles *Times,* December 9, 1941.

26. Bert Webber, *Silent Siege: Japanese Attacks Against North America in World War 2* (Fairfield, Washington: Ye Galleon Press, 1984), pp. 105–111.

27. Los Angeles *Times,* February 25, 1942.

28. Webber, *Silent Siege*, pp. 111–115; *Jack Smith's L.A.* (New York: McGraw-Hill, 1980), pp. 90–94.

29. Bob Hope and Melvin Shavelson, *Don't Shoot, It's Only Me* (New York: Jove Books, 1991), p. 64.

30. Bruce R. Lively, "Naval and Marine Corps Reserve Center, Los Angeles," *Southern California Quarterly,* vol. LXIX (Fall 1987), pp. 241, 254.

31. Los Angeles *Times,* April 12, 1992.

32. Ibid., August 30, 1942.

33. Ibid., August 8, 1942.

34. Ibid., April 6, 1992.

Democracy Abroad—Segregation at Home

3

While the war effort brought forth a spirit of cooperation and participation among Los Angeles citizens, serious undercurrents of racial tension continued to plague the region during the war years. Despite its long history as a migratory center, Los Angeles remained a city divided and segregated along racial lines. And while the American war effort promoted the ideals of spreading democracy abroad, minorities in wartime Los Angeles still found themselves contending with job discrimination, housing restrictions and public facilities use prohibitions.

In the wake of Japan's attack on Pearl Harbor, the city's Japanese-American community quickly found itself under siege. Large-scale raids on the community conducted by local police and F.B.I. authorities on the afternoon and evening of December 7 resulted in the forced detention of more than 1,300 Japanese-Americans.[1] As leaders of the Japanese-American community protested their innocence and noncomplicity in the attack on Pearl Harbor, several local political leaders, including Congressman Leland Ford of Los Angeles, nonetheless clamored for their removal from the Pacific coast. In response to being made "scapegoats" for the attack on Pearl Harbor, local Japanese-Americans found themselves defending their ancestry, their loyalty to the United States, and their right to remain in Los Angeles.

At first the plight of local Japanese-Americans received a sympathetic response from both the Los Angeles County Board of Supervisors and City Mayor Fletcher Bowron.[2] But as the early tide of the Pacific war continued to turn against the United States, and news reports disclosed recurring attacks and sinking of American maritime ships off the west coast by Japanese submarines, support for the local Japanese community began crumbling. The influential Los Angeles *Times*, for example, which in the early days following the attack on Pearl Harbor had advised its readership against prejudicial attitudes towards the city's Japanese community, soon took to calling these same citizens "Japs" and "Nips." Mayor Bowron was no better. He publicly announced that the rights of Japanese-Americans would be respected only one day after approving the removal of all Japanese-Americans from the city's payroll.[3] And by December 22, 1941, the Los Angeles Chamber of Commerce, which had previously advised its

Mayor Bowron welcoming a delegation of the city's Japanese-American community in August 1941. Within six months the mayor would be calling for the community's ouster from Los Angeles. (Photograph courtesy of the University of Southern California's Regional History Center).

membership to fight against the prevailing "war hysteria," quietly advised its Washington bureau to lobby California congressmen in support of Japanese relocation.[4]

In response to growing public pressure, in large part fueled by newspaper reports of purported espionage rings run by local Japanese citizens, the Los Angeles County Board of Supervisors voted unanimously on January 27, 1942 in favor of a resolution supporting the removal of Japanese aliens from Los Angeles. However, the failure of the resolution to include American-born Japanese in the expulsion order drew an angry rebuke from Los Angeles County District Attorney John Dockweiler who complained, "You can't tell the difference between a Jap, whether he is native born or a citizen.... We have got to make a drive to do something about American born Japs, not the alien Jap, but the American born."

Dockweiler warned, "He is the danger. He is the smart guy, he is the fellow who went back to Japan and learned his tricks there."[5]

The Southern California relocation plan quickly attracted regional and national attention. A growing chorus of political and military leaders put their weight behind the idea of relocating all persons of Japanese descent from the Pacific coast region, regardless of status or citizenship. The commander in charge of the defense of the western region of the United States, General James L. De Witt of the Western Defense Command concluded bluntly, "The Japanese race is an enemy race." Admitting that while "many second and third generation Japanese born on United States soil, possessed of United States citizenship, have become 'Americanized,' the racial strains," he avowed, remain "undiluted.... It therefore follows that along the vital Pacific Coast over 112,000 potential enemies, of Japanese extraction, are at large today."[6]

Declaring that "each of our little Japanese friends will know his part in the event of any possible attempted invasion or air raid," Bowron clamored for the removal of Japanese and Japanese-Americans from Los Angeles in February 1942. (Photograph courtesy of the University of Southern California's Regional History Center).

As fears mounted, Los Angeles Mayor Bowron with strong local support demanded that the federal government take immediate action against the local Japanese-American community before, in his words, "it is too late." In a February 5, 1942 radio address, Bowron stated that Los Angeles, with the nation's largest concentration of Japanese, had become, "the hotbed, the nerve center of the spy system, of planning for sabotage." Warning his listeners that "each of our little Japanese friends will know his part in the event of any possible attempted invasion or air raid," Bowron argued in support of plans that would remove all persons of Japanese descent from the city. Otherwise, he told his radio audience, "We are the ones who will be the human sacrifices."[7]

Bowron's sentiments only too accurately reflected the public's mood. Tensions had become so great that many Chinese-American residents took to wearing red, white and blue buttons to distinguish themselves from their embattled Japanese neighbors.[8] One local Chinese restaurateur went so far as to draft a series of guidelines for "native Americans" outlining the ethnic differences between the two groups. "The Chinese," he pointed out, "don't try to put on impressive faces." By contrast, "Japanese walk and talk faster," he wrote, and are rarely seen "strolling along in a relaxed manner." Further, "Japanese, outwardly, are more polite and very much more prone to bowings and scrappings."[9] In response to continued public pressure and demands for a complete removal of Japanese-Americans from the west coast by such political leaders as California Governor Culbert Olsen and California State Attorney General Earl Warren, President Franklin Delano Roosevelt took action. On February 19, 1942 he issued Executive Order 9066 which authorized the forcible evacuation of Japanese-Americans from the west coast. As a result, an estimated 60,000 Los Angeles Japanese-American residents were quickly forced out of their homes and businesses. Adding to the misery of losing their homes and livelihoods, Los Angeles Japanese-Americans were forced to live for two months in horse stables at both Santa Anita and Hollywood Park race tracks while the permanent internment camps were being constructed. This forced removal, which was one of the greatest large-scale violations of civil liberties in American history, stands out as a vivid reminder of racial tension and discrimination in Los Angeles during the war years.[10]

Although Los Angeles did not suffer from the pronounced racism found in the Deep South of the United States, overt and covert forms of prejudice and segregation were commonplace. Among the city's more common prejudicial practices were the listing of want ads that advertised

From the battlefield to a horse stall. Dressed in his uniform from World War I, an American veteran begins his internment at the Santa Anita Race Track assembly center. (Photograph courtesy of the National Archives)

for workers according to their religious beliefs. One example was a 1941 Los Angeles *Times* want ad that stated: "Col. Student desiring work for holidays. Must be good driver + typist. Highly recommended. Catholic Pref."[11]

Barring minorities from using public swimming facilities was an even more blatant form of discrimination. Pasadena's Brookside municipal swimming pool, for example, set a day aside in the week, called "International Day," for minorities barred from the facility on the other six days. At the close of the day, the pool's water was routinely drained and replaced before use by white customers.[12] And throughout Los Angeles, despite civil codes to the contrary, blacks were frequently refused rooms in hotels and often would not be served in restaurants unless they agreed to eat in the kitchen.[13]

So open and accepted were patterns of discrimination that newspapers offered guidelines for the payment of black help. For example, the feature page of *The Beverly Citizen* on March 22, 1940 dryly pointed out

A group of young internees plays marbles on the race track at Santa Anita in February 1942. (Photograph courtesy the National Archives)

that "Beverly Hills employers prefer, as a rule, the White domestic servant over the Colored," and then proceeded to list the average wages paid to Beverly Hills domestic servants, "White couples. . . $125 to $150, Colored couples. . . $100 to $125." The ease with which such practices found acceptance in Los Angeles created fears among members of the local chapter of the Urban League that blacks would suffer still further erosion of their position in the city as large numbers of white Southerners migrated to the area in search of defense industry employment. One observer of job opportunities for blacks during this period noted that, "The southernizing of California is becoming a real factor in mitigating against employment opportunities for the Negro... On all sides," he concluded, "can be sensed a general change of attitude toward the Negro, due to the impress of this southern influence on almost every activity within the community."[14]

The threat of job losses for blacks and the subsequent growth of racial impediments prompted Floyd C. Covington, Director of the Los Angeles Urban League, to make the harsh assessment in May 1940 that, "California is reliving almost identically the same experiences that imprinted the historical South during the slave period."[15]

Blacks migrating to California in search of work in the expanding war industries incurred the wrath of such nativist-oriented groups as the Native Sons of the Golden West and the California Joint Immigration Committee. With the Japanese problem "solved," these two groups shifted their focus from anti-Asian xenophobia to the perils of black migration to California. Resentment against blacks grew to such an extent that in 1944 Alexander R. Heron, California's Director of Rehabilitation and Reemployment, stated that there was greater prejudice against blacks on the west coast than there had been against persons of Japanese ancestry. Los Angeles writer Carey McWilliams concurred, observing, "there was much more resentment of Negro migrants than there was of evacuees."[16]

Although the boom in war production started as early as 1940, the wartime migration of large numbers of blacks to Los Angeles did not begin until the spring of 1942. The Southern Pacific Railroad Company, in need of track maintenance workers, recruited over 3,000 Southern blacks. This and similar recruitment drives brought blacks into the city at a peak rate of over 300 to 400 per day.[17] But conditions for these migrant workers were often harsh. Many recruits, found unfit for work due to poor health, were left without resources to return home. Others were forced to sleep without shelter, on railway roadbeds. Many of the migrants were never told about the nature of their work or the wages they would be paid. In turn, many new arrivals ran away and only later informed government investigators that they did so because the railroad employers failed to "treat them like human beings."[18] Moreover, Los Angeles authorities discovered that many of the recruited Southern blacks were underage. According to Dorothy Smith, Executive Secretary of the Travelers Aid Society, the situation proved problematic since "this city does not have any institutions which are suitable for the care of Negro boys of that age. There is no boys lodge or club for Negro boys." In the end, the Southern Pacific Railroad retained only a few of the Southern blacks it recruited for its track maintenance program, hiring Mexican nationals instead.[19]

Prior to the mass migration of blacks in 1942, black workers found themselves competing unsuccessfully for jobs with large numbers of white migrants, lured to the state by the promise of the highest wage and salary levels in the nation. While these white workers availed themselves of California's golden opportunities, black workers ran up against the wall of a defense industry reluctant to hire them. One observer of Los Angeles' black migration noted sadly that "education and skills were often seen as of little consequence because of institutional and individual racism."[20]

The failure of most Los Angeles defense plants to hire blacks can be traced to the attitudes of both organized labor and management. By restricting its initiation ritual to whites only, the aircraft industry's principal union, the AFL International Association of Machinists, barred blacks from membership until 1942.[21] Management policies were equally restrictive. When members of the Los Angeles Council of the National Negro Congress inquired about the racial policies of Vultee Aircraft in August 1940, Gerald Tuttle, manager of industrial relations for the company sent a curt reply: "I regret to say that it is not the policy of this company to employ people other than of the Caucasian race, consequently, we are not in a position to offer your people employment at this time."[22]

In Pasadena, the director of the California State Employment Service declared that his office was continually approached by competent black mechanics desiring work in the aircraft industry. Although the black mechanics often possessed the very skills the firms were looking for, the

As the male work force continued to be depleted by the war effort, millions of women marched into the nation's war industries to do their part for an Allied victory. Their consuming "can do" spirit helped to lift the nation's morale. (Photograph courtesy of the National Archives)

vast majority could not be placed. The personnel representative of a large aircraft plant admitted that although the company had hired many thousands of men in the previous year and was still in desperate need of skilled workers, "there isn't a Negro in the entire plant." The company's racial policy was in force, he wrote, because "many of the white men would object to working with a Negro."[23]

In the spring of 1941 J.H. Kindelberger, president of North American Aviation, issued a statement declaring that,

"While we are in complete sympathy with the Negroes, it is against the Company policy to employ them as mechanics or aircraft workers.... There will be some jobs as janitors for Negroes." He was firm however that, "Regardless of their training as aircraft workers, we will not employ them in the North American plant."[24]

For blacks in Los Angeles and for that matter throughout the nation, the incongruity of fighting a war for democratic ideals abroad while maintaining segregationist policies at home led to large-scale protests. The most successful of these protests was ironically a march that was never held. The proposed march, organized by black leader A. Philip Randolph, was to have brought more than 50,000 blacks demanding equal rights to Washington D.C. on July 1, 1941. The march was called off when President Franklin D. Roosevelt met with Randolph and agreed to issue an executive order outlawing discrimination.

Roosevelt's Executive Order 8802, issued June 25, 1941, forbade "discrimination in the employment of workers in defense industries or government because of race, creed, color or national origin." Roosevelt created the Committee on Fair Employment Practices (FEPC) to enforce the order.

In Los Angeles, which even prior to the Great Depression had a substantial black community, black protest between 1940—1942 garnered strength as many area blacks united together under the "Double V" campaign.[25] National in scope, the "Double V" campaign signified black America's efforts to win victory over the Axis powers overseas and over discrimination at home. To help attain these ends a variety of black organizations worked together documenting instances of discrimination against minorities in the work place. And the newly formed FEPC held two days of hearings in October 1941 on racial barriers to employment in Los Angeles' defense plants.

With expectations high in the black community that the FEPC involvement would alleviate discrimination in the region's war industries,

Charlotta Bass, editor and publisher of the black newspaper, the California *Eagle,* cautioned that "Negroes must not raise their hopes too high, for, with all its aura of federal authority, the FEPC has little real power." The problem, Bass noted, was that the FEPC had no authority to halt the production of vitally needed defense equipment in order to overturn discriminatory practices against black workers.[26]

Although the FEPC hearings did serve to raise the consciousness of the Southern California public about the reality of racial discrimination in the region's defense industries, black organizations had to continue to wage an uphill fight for the hiring of minorities by defense contractors. The Negro Victory Committee, formed in April 1941 was among the most successful of such black advocacy groups. Acting as an umbrella organization the Victory Committee adopted what historian E. Fredrick Anderson has called a "mainstream patriotic strategy." This strategy sought to remind the city's white majority of the American black community's historic loyalty to the nation while at the same time aggressively pursuing the cause of equal rights.[27]

At the heart of the organization's success was the work of Rev. Clayton D. Russell, who served as the Victory Committee's chairperson. Rev. Russell was a man of wide cultural and political experience. Educated in Los Angeles area schools, Russell had studied theology in Copenhagen, Denmark in the early 1930s at the International College. His experiences abroad profoundly influenced his thinking about the plight of blacks in America. Among such experiences was a tour of pre-war Germany where the Los Angeles cleric witnessed first-hand the rise of Adolph Hitler's National Socialist (Nazi) Party and its racist ideology. The eventual Nazi triumph in Germany made Russell keenly aware of what a German victory in the war would mean for American blacks.[28]

Russell's standing in the black community was further enhanced by the fact that he was the first black minister in Los Angeles to host his own radio program. As historian E. Frederick Anderson has observed, "Being on the radio in 1941 conferred instant celebrity status. For a black man to be on the radio was extraordinary." One of Russell's listeners remarked,

> People who came during the Depression and thereafter had been down by the system in the South. Clayton Russell's radio program, 'The Visitor' which came on every Sunday, gave them hope because he was the only Negro on the radio.... He had the audacity to make demands on the white power structure and told people what he was going to do. He had a ready-made audience, because you could hear the Visitor all over the black community on a Sunday morning.[29]

Russell helped to unify blacks in fighting discrimination. Under his leadership, the Negro Victory Committee organized five black-owned markets into the Victory Markets Cooperative. The cooperative functioned throughout the war years, helping to solidify black support behind both the war effort and their own fight for equality at home.

Black solidarity against hiring discrimination also received strong support from the community's two leading black newspapers, the California *Eagle* and the Los Angeles *Sentinel*.[30] Discrimination against blacks in Los Angeles also received national attention from *Fortune* magazine. In its March 1943 issue it accused Los Angeles defense plants of "almost universal prejudice against Negroes" with "little concealment about the anti-Negro policy."[31] And as Historian James Wilburn has noted, "In June, 1941 there were exactly four Negro production workers in the aircraft industry in Southern California."[32]

The black solidarity forged by Russell and other leaders soon became evident on the streets. In July 1942, a Los Angeles official of the United States Employment Service tried to justify discriminatory hiring practices by claiming that black women were not interested in working in defense production. The official went on to allege that black women, in his view, were better suited for work as domestic servants and cooks. The statement awakened long smoldering resentments in the black community where unemployment was severe despite the region's massive shortage of war workers.

In response, the Negro Victory Committee quickly mobilized hundreds of black women to flood the agency with job applications. A protest march organized by the committee led to public debate, and finally, to serious negotiations between the Victory Committee and various government officials, especially a group of federal officials from the War Manpower Commission. A joint statement was later issued by the negotiators stating that discrimination would no longer be tolerated in the defense industry.[33]

The Victory Committee's march played a paramount role in breaking down the barriers that had confronted blacks in the defense industry. Although Executive Order 8802 forbade discriminatory hiring practices, leaders throughout the black community felt the only hope for enforcement of the order was strong public pressure by blacks. Having come from the position of "we want to aid in the war effort but are prevented from doing so," the Negro Victory Committee avoided charges of subversion and anti-Americanism.

Fortunately for blacks and other minorities, Los Angeles began to suffer acute labor shortages in 1942. The aircraft industry, for example, had nearly 20,000 workers who either enlisted in or were drafted into the military by August 1942. Further, industrial expansion in the Los Angeles area between 1940 and mid-1943 accounted for the creation of 550,000 new jobs. Faced with this, defense industry employers were forced to hire from groups previously excluded, such as the physically disabled, women, and racial minorities.

The sudden change in fortune did not end the problems of blacks seeking war work. Despite by-laws to the contrary many labor unions remained opposed to hiring from these groups. In the shipyards in Los Angeles, for example, a bitter union fight broke out between black and white war workers.[34] Although the shipyards were the largest wartime employer of local blacks, the yard's Boilermaker's Union refused to accept blacks as union members. Adding insult to injury the black employees were nonetheless still forced to pay union dues. These policies earned the wrath of the Los Angeles Negro Victory Committee. When faced with growing racial tensions in the yards and the threat of large-scale black

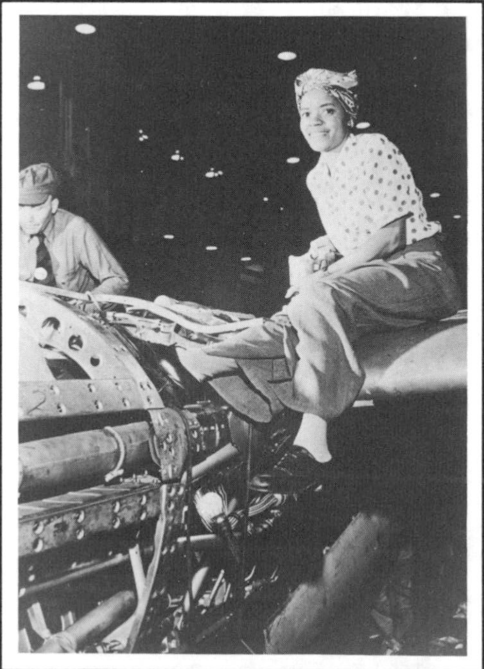

A proud riveter at Lockheed's Burbank aircraft plant. (Photograph courtesy of the National Archives)

protest, the Boilermakers relented somewhat and set up an auxiliary union local for the black workers. [35]

This attempt to appease the black shipyard workers did not obviate the fact that blacks were still required to pay dues to a union that discriminated against them. Upset that they were forced to work in segregated work gangs and that their black auxiliary remained under white supervision and control, black shipyard workers in Los Angeles formed the Shipyard Workers Committee for Equal Participation in the Unions.[36]

In response to growing complaints from the Shipyard Workers Committee, the FEPC sent an investigating team to the west coast in the summer of 1943. Walter Williams, the president of the Shipyard Workers Committee, warned that the situation in Los Angeles had deteriorated to the point that a race riot could break out. The team, led by James Wolfe, then Chief Justice of the Utah Supreme Court, and FEPC representative Daniel Donovan, concurred. Their report to the FEPC office in Washington D.C. stated that blatant racist practices found throughout shipyards on the west coast would be for the FEPC, "the biggest question it will perhaps handle during its whole existence."[37]

The problem was so acute that the FEPC was forced to continue their investigative and enforcement work throughout the war. Although the FEPC itself had been revamped and strengthened under Roosevelt's Executive Order 9346 in May 1943, the Boilermakers Union remained a formidable and defiant foe. However, given that federal defense contracts had become the source of the shipyard's bread and butter, company owners sought to come to terms with Roosevelt's Executive Order and other subsequent FEPC requests.[38]

Encouraged by the FEPC's efforts, black shipyard workers themselves began filing suits against the Boilermakers Union. The most important of these was *James v. Marinship Corporation* (1944). The California State Supreme Court ruled against the union on every count and affirmed lower court rulings that segregated and discriminatory unions were illegal in California.[39] Still, this ruling and others like it were circumvented by the union. The Boilermakers, for example, abolished the auxiliary status of black locals but kept white and black locals separate in structure. Consequently the union was able to continue the practice of assigning jobs based on race.[40] In the words of one observer, "The union had altered the form but retained the substance of its nationwide system of anti-Negro practices."[41]

In the aircraft industry the lack of closed-shop agreements put the burden of hiring blacks on the shoulders of management. As with the shipyards, growing shortages of workers, in conjunction with black protest and threatened government reprisals, forced the aircraft plant owners to hire black workers. While some plants were slow in implementing a non-discrimination policy, others, such as Lockheed-Vega, used their company newspaper to explain its intent to carry out the provisions of Roosevelt's Executive Order 8802.[42]

The change in management policy put the unions in an awkward position. The growing number of black workers entering the industry could provide unions strength through increased membership or it could hemorrhage it internally over race-oriented disputes. As a result, the CIO and some local AFL unions became increasingly outspoken against discrimination. Although the record for each aircraft industry union varied both the AFL and CIO eventually took important steps to improve the rights of black workers.[43]

Despite apparent gains made by blacks in defense hiring, the fact remains that they received a disproportionately small share of jobs when compared to their population. In June 1944 blacks composed 5.3 percent of the war workers in Los Angeles yet blacks constituted 7.1 percent of the city's population.[44]

The open hiring of blacks in the high-paying defense industry led to the greatest black migration in Los Angeles history. By the summer of 1943 blacks were arriving in Los Angeles at a rate of between 10,000 to 12,000 a month, or approximately fifty percent of new migrants to the city.[45] From 55,114 in 1940, the black population of Los Angeles swelled to 118,888 by April 1944.[46]

The mass migration exacerbated the problems of local blacks as the record numbers of migrants increased competition for defense jobs and scarce wartime housing. Because the black community was forcibly segregated by racial covenants to approximately 5 per cent of the city's residential area, newly arriving blacks had great difficulty in finding housing within the established black communities of Central Avenue, West Jefferson, and Watts.[47] Many of the newly arrived migrants were forced to live instead in the city's "Little Tokyo" section which had been emptied because of the internment of Japanese-Americans. Renamed by locals as "Bronzeville," this section was considered to be the worst wartime housing in Los Angeles. Deputy City Mayor Caldwell was so appalled at the conditions there that he testified to federal investigators that if they visited the area, as he had, "You will see life as no human is expected to endure it." A member of the Los Angeles Women's War Chest Committee echoed Caldwell's sentiments stating that the conditions in "Bronzeville," "almost require the help of missionaries."[48]

Adding to the black community's wartime woes was the lack of adequate public transportation to and from employment sites. The issue proved especially volatile among black migrants given that most of the new arrivals could not afford cars, but were forced to live in segregated areas often distant from the defense plants. Los Angeles' key public transportation system, the Los Angeles Railway Corporation's inter-urban transportation network, relied on street cars and buses to provide service throughout the city. However, with the outbreak of the war, the system's already inadequate service to minority communities was further hindered by the lack of operators, many of whom had joined the military or left the organization for higher-paying positions in war production work. By December 1942 more than three hundred street cars and buses, capable of carrying upwards of 30,000 Los Angeles war workers, remained idle due to lack of operators. Yet despite the great shortage of operators, the Los Angeles Railway Corporation refused to hire blacks or Hispanics as motormen or conductors. The discriminatory policy became a rallying point in the black community.

In its fight with the Los Angeles Railway Corporation the Negro Victory Committee organized a large bond raising rally in December 1942. Held in the city's Pershing Square, the rally featured numerous black entertainers, including Ethel Walters, Clarence Muse and Noble Sissle. Throughout the well-attended patriotic rally the audience was informed that the Los Angeles Railway Corporation impeded the war effort by allowing hundreds of transportation vehicles to remain idle without giving minority Americans a chance to operate them. Organizers apparently hit a special chord as many frustrated white commuters supported the bond drive's dual cause of helping American troops abroad and getting public transportation to function properly in Los Angeles. According to the California *Eagle*, the bond drive's success could be measured by large white audience participation that helped the rally sell over 62,000 war bonds.[49]

The Negro Victory Committee next met with leaders of the Los Angeles Railway Corporation to discuss minority hiring problems. The leaders of the Victory Committee pointed out that they had governmental legal protection through Executive Order 8802. Further, the Victory Committee argued it had the support of the company's AFL union leadership.

(This was accomplished by the Victory Committee supporting the union's demand for higher wages in turn for its support of minority hiring.) The end result of the meeting, according to Guy Nunn of the Minorities Division of the War Manpower Commission, was that "Negro motormen, conductors and conductorettes will be hired and upgraded by the Los Angeles Railway Company."[50]

On February 9, 1943 the Los Angeles Railway Corporation informed its workers that the company would comply with Executive Order 8802. Eight days later the company attempted to upgrade two of its black employees to apprentice mechanics. As a result white workers refused to go to work. The company, after failing twice to upgrade the two black employees, told the FEPC that the union was unable to end the work stoppages. In fact, by late 1943 the company complained it was the union that prevented it from hiring qualified black workers.[51]

By January 1, 1944 the situation had deteriorated to the point that only 493 streetcars of the normal 800 were in use and only 212 buses were in operation while 144 remained idle. When the FEPC held hearings on August 8, 1944 on the continuing problems of Los Angeles' public transportation system, it found that the company had made the union responsible for making white workers accept blacks although the union had played an active role in denying blacks jobs. The FEPC, buoyed by the federal government's seizure of the Philadelphia transit system only days earlier over issues similar to those in Los Angeles, ordered the company to desist from its discriminatory practices.[52] Fearing that the federal government would seize the Los Angeles Railway Corporation, workers and management capitulated to government demands and began hiring minorities as conductors and operators.[53]

Although the overall legacy for blacks in Los Angeles during the war years proved to be mixed, the political and organizational skills learned by the community would prove of lasting value. Among the accomplishments of the wartime civil rights movement were the gradual breaking down of racist barriers to civil service and defense industry employment. Further, during the war Los Angeles blacks took the lead in a successful fight to end the pre-war legal enforcement of racial housing covenants.

The Spanish-speaking community of wartime Los Angeles, estimated by researchers as 10 percent of the city's population, also confronted problems of discrimination and segregation.[54] Torn between a Spanish-based heritage and an English-speaking "Anglo" Los Angeles, Hispanics found themselves faced, in some unique ways, with difficult questions of cultural and racial identity. Anglo society made its contribution to the Hispanic cultural dilemma. The United States government, for example, classified Hispanics as "whites" in the 1940 census. By contrast, several Los Angeles area school districts officially regarded Hispanics as "Indians."

In addition, generational gulfs had been opened between foreign-born parents and their American born off-spring. This was particularly true for those of Mexican ancestry. Second generation Mexican-Americans, raised in Anglo society, were characteristically more fluent in English than in their parent's Spanish. "They were," according to historian Gerald Nash, "suspended between two worlds—neither Anglo nor Mexican."[55]

Despite such problems, Spanish-speaking Americans distinguished themselves in the war effort, both at home and abroad. More than 450,000 Hispanics served in the American armed forces. Conspicuously, seventeen Congressional Medals of Honor acknowledged their exemplary war record.[56] On the homefront, Hispanics worked within the prevailing social system to correct inequitable racial policies and practices. And despite numerous setbacks in the fight for racial justice, Spanish-speaking Americans remained loyal to the nation's cause.

In Los Angeles' Mexican-American community, "Reform, not revolution" characterized efforts to change the racial status quo.[57] Especially proud that Los Angeles had the largest percentage of Mexican-Americans in the armed forces of any city in the nation, Hispanic leaders, like their black counterparts, stressed that by working in prevailing institutions, democratic ideals, both at home and abroad could be realized. It was not uncommon to see numerous American flags flying throughout the barrio of East Los Angeles during the war years.

However, despite attempts at cultural integration, the Second World War represented a time of marked racial tension in the Mexican-American community.[58] Much of this involved young second generation Mexican-Americans, who were estranged from their parents' conservative Mexican ways and the Anglo society that refused to regard them as equals. Difficulties in school, run-ins with police, frustrations with limited job prospects left many young Mexican-Americans directionless. Frustrated, many banded together in cliques or gangs. While some cliques, called "palomillias," were purely social, others known as "pachucos" displayed classic antisocial behavior. Although pachucos were a distinct minority among Mexican-American youth, they tended to attract attention.[59]

Pachucos developed their own slang, social structure and mores. They gained public visibility through adopting an exaggerated style of dress, donning what later became known to Angelenos during the war as a "zoot suit." The zoot suit consisted of a long coat, a pancake hat, pants with narrow cuffs and pointed shoes. The "pachucos," or "chucos," as they liked to call themselves, also wore their hair long but slicked back into a ducktail.[60]

In wartime Los Angeles, the pachucos provoked a strong public reaction. Many Angelenos took offense at the extravagance of the pachuco clothing in a time of shortages and sacrifice. War jitters, exacerbated by the city's growing crime rate, served to focus public attention on the pachuchos. Unfortunately, other, often innocent Mexican-American youths, were arrested in vigorous police campaigns against juvenile delinquents in the crime ridden barrios.

In the first week of August 1942, gang conflict resulted in two murders and a number of assaults. Los Angeles police acted swiftly. In one large raid, which the Los Angeles *Times* called, "the biggest roundup since prohibition days," officers arrested more than three hundred Mexican-American youths.[61] The large-scale police operation was precipitated by the discovery of the unconscious body of Jose Diaz near a swimming hole in East Los Angeles where a gang fight had occurred. The man's subsequent death led to the filing of murder charges against twenty-two gang members. The criminal trial which followed gripped public attention, entering the annals as the Sleepy Lagoon Murder case.[62]

The coming trial rapidly heightened tensions between the Mexican-American community and the city at large. The media and several police authorities played up the alleged racial characteristics of the gang members as they attempted to prove that Mexican-Americans, as a group, had a propensity toward crime. At one point a sheriff's official stated that juvenile delinquency among Mexican-American youth was basically biological and that "one cannot change the spots of a leopard."[63] The ensuing mass trial garnered national attention. In the end, the court found three of the defendants guilty of first degree murder; nine were convicted of second-degree murder and five were convicted on lesser charges. Five of the 22 youths were acquitted on all counts.[64]

The trial galvanized the Mexican-American community in Los Angeles and resulted in the formation of the Sleepy Lagoon Defense Committee. Seeking to appeal the convictions, the committee won the support of several major Hollywood stars who helped to raise money for a defense fund. Prominent among these was Orson Welles who declared, "After a very careful examination of the records and facts of the trial, I am convinced that the boys in the Sleepy Lagoon case were not given a fair trial, and that their convictions could only have been influenced by anti-Mexican prejudice."[65]

In October 1944, the District Court of Appeals reversed the guilty verdicts, citing lack of evidence and the prejudicial conduct of the trial judge. Writer Carey McWilliams reflecting on the case stated, "I wouldn't say the zoot suiters were mother's angels but they weren't devils, either. The papers were dreadful. The officials no better."[66]

The problems of youth gangs in the barrios attracted efforts at reform. Young Mexican-American professionals, led by bilingual attorney Manuel Ruiz, Jr., formed the Coordinating Council for Latin-American Youth in hopes that the Mexican-American community and Anglo organizations could work together to solve the problems which gave rise to juvenile delinquency in the barrio. Similarly, the Los Angeles Grand Jury set up the Special Committee on the Problems of Mexican Youth which boasted among its members Guy Nunn of the War Manpower Commission, Manuel Aguiliar, the Mexican Associate Consul, and author Carey McWilliams.[67]

In its 1942 report to the County Grand Jury, the committee pointed out, "young people of Mexican ancestry have been more sinned against than sinning, in discriminations and limitations that have been placed on them and their families." Among the committee's recommendations were judgments that discrimination against Mexican-Americans in public places such as playgrounds and swimming pools be abolished, and that the Board of Education provide adequate vocational programs for Mexican youth. The committee also then demanded that local health and housing authorities take immediate steps to alleviate the deplorable conditions then prevalent throughout the Mexican-American community.[68]

However, despite the attempts to discourage gang membership, the pachuco trademark—the zoot suit—grew in popularity among young Mexican-American males. And while the vast majority of the young Mexican-Americans had little if anything to do with the pachucos, public perception identified zoot suiters with gangs and criminal activity. On the night of June 3, 1943 large-scale fighting broke out between the zoot suiters and servicemen. While the tension between the two groups had been mounting for some time, the exact origins of zoot suit riots are unclear; however racism played a large part in instigating the violence. The uniforms of each group seemed to take on meaning. Many servicemen saw the zoot suit as a symbol of open defiance of society. Further, many military personnel considered the zoot suiters draft dodgers. In contrast, many of the zoot suiters resented the constant traffic of servicemen through their neighborhoods and the attention the servicemen gave to their girlfriends. For some Mexican-Americans, the military uniforms symbolized dominant Anglo society invading their closed world.

While no one was killed during the riots, police were unable to control the mobs of servicemen who swarmed into the downtown area in search of zoot suiters. Their invasion was precipitated by rumors that Mexican hoodlums had openly attacked servicemen near a dance hall in Venice on the night of June 3, 1943. For at least ten days military officials were unable to control the servicemen despite efforts by local and military police authorities. There were simply too many service personnel involved in the riots to be controlled. The rioters marched through the downtown area stripping zoot suiters of their outfits. They even entered a movie theatre, turned on the lights, and attacked persons they considered to be zoot suiters. Most of the victims were Mexican-Americans, but there were cases of attacks on blacks as well. The riots stopped after the commanding officers of Southern California military bases put the barrio and downtown areas on off-limits status.[69]

The zoot suit riots made international news. Both the Mexican government and the United States State Department became involved, putting pressure on military authorities to control their personnel. Embarrassed officials in Los Angeles sought to open up communication with the region's Hispanics. Both the city and county governments formed task forces to increase understanding between the Anglo and Hispanic cultures. While these efforts were a strong improvement over past policies, Hispanics throughout the war faced exclusion and discrimination.

Like the black, Hispanics resided in neighborhoods and attended schools segregated from white society. Even by 1946 there were still twenty-eight separate schools in Los Angeles County for Mexican-American children. School districts drew boundary lines down the center of streets without including dwellings on either side to connect settlements of Hispanics into segregated school districts.[70] Forced into segregated and most often inferior housing districts as well, Hispanics coped with overcrowding and poor sanitary conditions throughout the war years.

In the area of employment, records of the wartime FEPC show that Hispanics faced discrimination in all but unskilled jobs.[71] While in many cases opposition to the employment of Hispanics was not as harsh as it was for blacks, discrimination against Hispanics was commonplace in wartime Los Angeles.

Often, however, the plight of Hispanics was the same as that of blacks. Both groups gained employment in many occupations only when large labor shortages afflicted the region. When Hispanics were hired, it was often in second tier positions. Labor unions, too, forced Hispanics into separate auxiliaries since many national charters were restricted to "Caucasian" membership. The FEPC declared in its *Final Report* that during the war discrimination against Mexican-Americans paralleled that against black workers.[72]

Despite problems of racism, the Hispanics of Los Angeles made gains during the Second World War. While the "zoot suit" riots appeared to have created the necessary attention to the plight of young Mexican-Americans, grass-root community organizations in the Mexican-American community began a constructive dialogue between themselves and Anglo society. In their fight against racism, Hispanic community leaders organized large-scale support throughout their neighborhoods. By keeping their goals tied to democratic ideals while preaching "reform and not revolution," the Hispanic community garnered political recognition and strength accelerating its acculturation into American society, while retaining ties to its ethnic heritage.[73]

In conclusion, the onset of the war exacerbated the problems of discrimination and segregation that had historically been present in Los Angeles. While the war did not dramatically alter these practices, minority groups, nonetheless, made significant gains, the most important of which involved federal recognition of the plight of minorities. Although many federal programs did little to advance the cause of minorities, other policies, such as those related to nondiscriminatory hiring on federally contracted war projects, significantly helped to break down employment barriers. As a result many minorities were able to advance beyond jobs to which they had historically been delegated. Those that were able to accomplish this had the salutary effect of making themselves into important role models for others in their community.

Another important advance in the fight for equal rights was the rise of minority-led grass-roots community organizations. In Los Angeles, many such groups emerged to take advantage of the racially more open climate occasioned by the war. The most successful of these organizations attached themselves to the country's own political agenda, the democratic ideals promoted by the Second World War. By working through the "system," many grass-roots organizations were highly effective in fighting racism and discrimination throughout the city, particularly in the vital areas of hiring policy and housing. Community organizations also laid the groundwork for concerted political action by minority groups, particularly at the ballot box.

Although the specific gains made by Los Angeles' racial minorities during the war years were admittedly limited, they nonetheless had a profound impact in shaping the future American civil rights movement. Further, the wartime inroads made against racial discrimination in the Southland served to significantly advance the cause of minorities in the fight for equal rights for all Americans.

Endnotes

1. In the four days following the attack on Pearl Harbor, 1,370 "suspicious" Japanese and Japanese-Americans were rounded-up in Los Angeles.
2. John Modell, *The Economics and Politics of Racial Accommodation: The Japanese of Los Angeles, 1900–1942 (Chicago:* University of Illinois Press, 1977), p. 183.
3. Regarding the dismissal of Japanese-Americans from Los Angeles City civil service positions see Los Angeles City Council file, 1942, CF 10483, Los Angeles City Archives.
4. Los Angeles *Times,* December 23, 1941.
5. As quoted in Modell, *The Economics and Politics of Racial Accommodation,* pp. 186–187.
6. U.S. Army, Western Defense Command and Fourth Army, *Final Report-Japanese Evacuation from the West Coast* (Washington, 1943), p. 34.
7. Radio speech given on February 5, 1942. Congressman John Costello inserted the speech in the *Congressional Record,* 77th Cong., 2nd sess. (1942), pp. 457–459. For a more thorough examination of Fletcher Bowron's role in the events leading up to the evacuation of the Japanese, see Morton Grodzins, *Americans Betrayed: Politics and the Japanese Evacuation* (Chicago: University of Chicago Press, 1949), pp. 100–106.
8. Los Angeles *Times,* December 19, 1941.
9. Ibid., December 28, 1941.
10. An excellent study of America's decision to evacuate the Japanese is Roger Daniels, *The Decision to Relocate the Japanese* (Malabar, FL: R.E. Krieger Publishing Company, 1975).
11. Los Angeles *Times,* December 21, 1941.
12. James E. Crimi, "The Social Status of the Negro in Pasadena, California" (Master's thesis, University of Southern California, 1941), p. 75.

13. Carnegie-Mydral Study, "Survey of the Negro," Form 7. Los Angeles Urban League Papers, Collection 203, Box 1, University of California, Los Angeles.
14. Carnegie-Mydral Study, Form 4.
15. Carnegie-Mydral Study, Form 1, p. 2.
16. Carey McWilliams, "Changing Aspects of the Evacuee Problem on the West Coast," *A Monthly Summary of Events and Trends in Race Relations* 2, (August-September, 1944), p. 21.
17. Lawrence Brooks de Graaf, "Negro Migration to Los Angeles, 1930 to 1950" (Ph.D. dissertation, University of California, Los Angeles, 1962), p. 262.
18. Transcript, "Negro Importation Hearing," July 14, 1942. Carey McWilliams Collection, Box 16, file 1. Special Collections, University of California, Los Angeles.
19. Ibid.
20. As quoted in Alonzo Nelson Smith, "Black Unemployment in the Los Angeles Area, 1938–1948" (Ph.D dissertation, University of California, Los Angeles, 1978), p. 49.
21. De Graaf, "Negro Migration to Los Angeles," p. 167.
22. As quoted in National Negro Congress, Los Angeles Council, *Jim Crow in National Defense* (Los Angeles, n.p., 1940), p. 13.
23. Crimi, "The Negro in Pasadena," pp. 38–39.
24. Lester B. Granger, "Negroes and War Production," *Survey Graphic* 31 (November 1942), p. 470.
25. A good summation of Los Angeles' substantial Black community before the Second World War can be found in Lawrence de Graaf's, "The City of Black Angels: Emergence of the Los Angeles Ghetto, 1890–1960," *Pacific Historical Review,* 39:3 (August 1970), pp. 323-352.
26. California *Eagle,* October 9, 1941.
27. E. Frederick Anderson, *The Development of Leadership and Organization Building in the Black Community of Los Angeles from 1900 Through World War II* (Saratoga: Twenty Century One Publishing, 1980), pp. 85–86.

28. Ibid., p. 87.

29. Ibid., p. 92.

30. Issues of the Los Angeles *Sentinel* are not available for the years 1941–45.

31. *Fortune Magazine* 23 (March 1943), p. 98.

32. James Wilburn, "The Aircraft Industry in Metropolitan Los Angeles During World War 2" (Ph.D. dissertation, University of California, Los Angeles, 1971), p. 165.

33. Anderson, Leadership and Organization Building in the Black *Community of Los Angeles,* pp. 88–91.

34. For comparison, in July 1944 there were 7,186 blacks employed in all of Los Angeles' aircraft industry. In December 1944 the California Shipbuilding Company and Consolidated Steelyards alone employed 7,022 blacks.

35. Anderson, *Leadership and Organization Building in the Black Community of Los Angeles,* p. 97.

36. William H. Harris, "Federal Intervention in Union Discrimination: F.E.P.C. and West Coast Shipyards During World War II" *Labor Herald* 22:3 (1981), p 331

37. Ibid., pp. 331–332.

38. Ibid., p. 341.

39. Ibid., pp. 343–345.

40. Fair Employment Practice Committee, *Final Report* (Washington, 1947), p. 21.

41. Herbert Hill, *Black Labor and the American Legal System: Race Work and the Law* (Wisconsin: University of Wisconsin Press, 1985), p. 206.

42. Wilburn, "The Aircraft Industry in Metropolitan Los Angeles During World War II," pp. 175–176.

43. Ibid., pp. 244–246.

44. Ibid., p. 270.

45. 78th Congress, first session, House, Subcommittee of Committee on Naval Affairs, *Hearings on Congested Areas* (8 parts, Washington, 1944), Part 8, p. 1761. (Hereafter cited as *Congested Area Hearings.*)

46. De Graaf, "Negro Migration to Los Angeles," p. 263.
47. Mignon E. Rothstein, "A Study of the Growth of Negro Population in Los Angeles and Available Housing Facilities Between 1940 and 1946," (Master's thesis, University of Southern California, 1950), pp. 36–44. In fact, as late as 1950 the United States Census showed that the city of Los Angeles contained 78 per cent of the blacks in the county.
48. *Congested Area Hearings,* Part 8, p. 1761.
49. *California Eagle,* December 25, 1942.
50. Quoted in Anderson, *Leadership and Organization Building in the Black Community of Los Angeles,* p. 96.
51. Hill, *Black Labor and the American Legal System,* p. 313.
52. Ibid., pp. 313–316.
53. Robert C. Weaver, *Negro Labor-A National Problem* (New York: Harcourt, Brace and Company, 1946), pp. 180–181.
54. Nash, *The American West Transformed,* p. 109.
55. Ibid., p. 110.
56. Ibid.
57. Mario T. Garcia, "Americans All: The Mexican American Generation and the Politics of Wartime Los Angeles," *Social Science Quarterly* 65:2 (June 1984), p. 279.
58. Ricardo Romo, *East Los Angeles: History of a Barrio* (Austin: University of Texas Press, 1983), p. 166.
59. Ibid.
60. Nash, *The American West Transformed,* pp. 110–111.
61. Los Angeles *Times,* August 10, 1942.
62. Romo, *East Los Angeles,* p. 166.
63. Quoted in Mauricio Mazon, *The Psycholoqy of Symbolic Annihilation: The Zoot-Suit Riots* (Austin: University of Texas Press, 1984), p. 22.
64. Romo, *East Los Angeles,* p. 166.
65. Quoted in Nash, *The American West Transformed,* p. 114.
66. Ibid.

67. Garcia, "Americans All," pp. 279–280.

68. *Report of Special Committee on Problems of Mexican Youth of the 1942 Grand Jury of Los Angeles County,* pp. 159–161.

69. For accounts of the "Zoot Suit Riots" see Mauricio Mazon, *The Psychology of Symbolic Annihilation: The Zoot Suit Riots;* Richard Romo, *East Los Angeles, pp. 165–167;* Gerald Nash, *The American West Transformed,* pp. 115–121.

70. Vesta Penrod, "Civil Rights Problems of Mexican-Americans in Southern California," (Master's thesis, Claremont Graduate School, 1948), pp. 49–50.

71. Ibid., p. 83.

72. Fair Employment Practice Committee, *Final Report,* p. 81.

73. Garcia, "Americans All," pp. 288.

Don't You Know There's a War Going On?

4

In the early months of the war a seemingly apocryphal story began sweeping the country. In Los Angeles, the story's version often involved two women sharing a seat on a street car. In making conversation one woman remarks to the other, "Well, my husband has a better job than he ever had and he's making more money, so I hope the war lasts a long time." With that, the other woman rises to her feet and slaps the offending woman across the face while blurting out, "That's for my boy who was killed at Pearl Harbor. And this," as she slaps her a second time, "is for my boy on Bataan."[1]

Much like the two women on the street car, the war forced a seemingly split personality on the citizenry of Los Angeles. On the one hand the war proved to be painfully close, as long casualty lists of local youth were read aloud at work gatherings and school assemblies. Adding to the gloom were seemingly endless newspaper and radio reports that carried news of horrific battles being fought in what had become history's bloodiest conflict. Yet, as the local citizenry continued to pray for its troops "over there," the city itself prospered as never before. Angelenos literally watched in amazement as familiar decade-old unemployment and bread lines gave way to bustling long lines of workers entering local defense plants. This dramatic change from economic depression to an abundance of work and money caused many Angelenos to feel guilty about their sudden change of fortune. The story of the two women on the street car was perhaps told throughout Los Angeles to remind everyday citizens of what the war was really about.

One young man who learned quickly about the war's impact was Santa Monica High School Math teacher Bob Crawford, who spied his friend and boss, Principal Pete Barnum, walking slowly back and forth in the school's otherwise empty outdoor amphitheater. Quietly observing from afar, Crawford watched as Barnum's walk came to a halt in front of the school's memorial wall. There the principal would stare at each of the names and then would slowly begin the walk again only to return minutes later to the wall. Tearfully recounting the memory, Crawford recalled that he saw the principal do it each morning and that Barnum's own health seemed to deteriorate as more names were added to the memorial wall.

Barnum's death a few months later would be attributed to the emotional toll the war took on the caring principal.

Evidence of the Second World War was decidedly pronounced throughout Los Angeles. Blackouts, carefully camouflaged industrial plants, and thousands of G. I.s roaming the city testified to the fact that the war was real and close. The local citizenry seemed to take the war in stride, openly welcoming the wounded, accepting without complaint the loud testing of hundreds of war planes overhead, and, as a show of support, turning up in large numbers to welcome badly damaged naval vessels returning from the Pacific war zone. [2] The war forged a pervasive sense of community spirit. The city's once fabled "everyone here is from somewhere else" gave way to an "all of us are in this together," spirit. Imbued with this sense of community, thousands of Angelenos proudly volunteered their services to local government and social service agencies.

As the large numbers of Angelenos worked alongside one another, from directing traffic to helping serve coffee at U.S.O. functions, another altogether different entity helped to further bond the people of Los Angeles together. As dusk settled over the city, the shared experience of preparing one's home for the evening blackout brought friends and neighbors together. As block wardens carefully checked each home's compliance, visiting neighbors and family members often gathered behind the darkened drapes to play parlor games or to listen to the radio. One woman recalled how as a young girl she looked forward to the city's first blackout. She recalled, "When the first one was announced, my girlfriend and I thought we were going to have lots of fun. We invited our boy friends over so we could sit in the dark and kiss and giggle. But we hadn't taken my mother into consideration. During the blackout we sat on the couch, as planned, but my mother sat in the middle. There we sat during the whole thing and nobody said a word because mother was watching, seeing to it that all the vestal virgins were protected."[3]

Also adjusting to life with blackouts were owners of golf driving ranges, baseball teams and amusement piers. Given their need for bright lights during evening hours, the golf ranges were forced to end their operations by dusk, causing many range owners to suffer steep declines in revenues. Local baseball team owners and fans fared somewhat better as evening games were moved, to the delight of pitchers, to twilight schedules at both Wrigley and Gilmore fields. While amusement pier operations were restricted during blackout proceedings, owners of the Venice and Ocean Park Amusement Piers were allowed to operate during periods of "dimout" as long as all of the piers' lights were shielded. One ride operator optimistically observed at the time, "We'll have 'dimout' rides now and I believe the young folks will like that."[4]

The advertising industry especially thrived under the new blackout restrictions. Local advertisers often walked a fine line, playing on the public's fear of an imminent Japanese attack while at the same time assuring their customers that use of a particular product would enhance the user's wartime safety. One hearing aid manufacturer, for example, attempted to boost its sales with the ad, "Until Blackouts came probably you thought you were 'getting by' with your hearing." Fire equipment companies also hoped for a financial bonanza by advertising such commodities as "Victory" fog nozzles for garden hoses. One local company promoted the "Bucket Pump," advertising that it was the "pump that saved London" during the German blitz of 1940.

More reassuring to the populace, however, were ads like those employed by the city's Ambassador Hotel. Under the banner, "To Aid in the Clearing of the Streets," the Ambassador offered stranded Angelenos free admission into its Ambassador Theatre and "Cocoanut Grove" night club for the duration of the blackout. Within the Class A Steel and concrete structure, potential guests were told they would not feel any "obligation to purchase food or beverages." The Santa Fe Cigar company also sought to alleviate its customer blackout fears by using the byline, "Lights out.... An ominous waiting quiet.... Carefully sheltered, you light a Santa Fe. Then, its dull glow will steadfastly endure, never to betray, but give you solace in the darkness."

One man who worried about a Japanese air attack, yet had a sense of gallows humor about it, was movie mogul Jack Warner. Fearing that his Burbank movie studio might be mistaken by Japanese planes for the nearby Lockheed Aircraft plant, Warner had his set painters emblazon on a sound stage roof a large arrow pointing towards the aircraft plant and the large block letters, LOCKHEED—THATAWAY, carefully spelled out. Warner shortly had the letters painted over, remarking that in light of the war's bloodshed, that the roof sign was no longer, "funny."[5]

Many in Los Angeles simply adjusted to the war's presence with as a little inconvenience as possible. Rather than give into the Pacific coast war threat, for example, organizers of the 1942 Rose Bowl football game simply moved the popular event to Durham, North Carolina. [6] Also adjusting were evening driver's travelling along the city's Pacific Coast Highway who quickly learned to drive with just their parking lights on at speeds no faster than fifteen miles an hour. School age children found themselves being taught and tested on first aid techniques. And Angelenos of all ages often found themselves carefully tending, many for the first time, fruits and vegetables in their own backyard "Victory Gardens."

Some Angelenos, however, seemed to have adjusted too well to the war's onset. Particularly stunned at the activities of wartime Los Angeles were numerous emigres from what was now a war-torn Europe. One particularly distraught observer was Austrian emigré writer Salka Viertel, who seeing apparently indifferent Americans relaxing in the sun, complained of, "the unconcerned sunbathers on the beach, their hairless bodies glistening and brown."[7] Echoing her disbelief was German refugee Carl Zuckmayer. Having just escaped Hitler's Germany, he angrily wrote of a Christmas party that he attended at the Beverly Hills Hotel. Describing the experience he wrote, "A slide had been covered with artificial snow and men in bathing trunks, women in silk jerseys, skied down it directly into the cocktail tent. Huge crimson poinsettias bloomed in all the gardens. The sight of all this nauseated me. "[8]

In truth while such sights as, "the supermarkets with their mountains of food," stunned arrivals like Salka Viertel, the war was never really far from the minds of most Angelenos. Los Angeles *Times* columnist, Lee Shippey, struck a cord with many of his readers when he shared the story of his regular attendance at a newsreel theatre. He wrote, "Several times I noticed a sweet old lady there. Yesterday she smiled and spoke as I came out. 'I wonder if you're coming for the same reason I do,' she said. 'I have a boy 'over there' and I keep hoping to glimpse his face on the screen."[9]

The war for Angelenos was all too real as evidenced by capacity bearing military hospitals located throughout the city. The beaches, too, were not filled by "unconcerned sunbathers" but more often provided solace for battle hardened troops on leave. South of the Santa Monica Pier, for example, once swank beach clubs were taken over by the military as rest and relaxation centers for war-worn fliers, many of whom had over fifty missions under their belts. The Army used other sections of the popular beach as recreational areas for troops soon to be sent to the South Pacific. And exhausted war workers, too, found temporary respite from the war using the warm quiet sands as a place to catch up on much needed sleep. Interestingly, many using Santa Monica Beach did so under the protective gaze of female lifeguards since the majority of Santa Monica's male lifeguards had been called into military service by the middle of 1942.[10]

Still wartime abuses, especially in the area of gas rationing, did occur. Federal officials repeatedly complained to the mayor's office that city-owned automobiles, which were not subject to gas and tire rationing, were being routinely used by city employees for the purpose of "night club hopping."[11] Several medical doctors, too, whose cars also were not subject to rationing, found themselves under public scrutiny when newspaper photographs were taken of their vehicles outside the horse racing track at Santa Anita. Somewhat more humorous was the activity of several young boys, who on the eve of their entering military service decided to syphon gas for a last trip together to the nearby mountains of Big Bear. Feeling too guilty to syphon gas from their neighbor's cars in Santa Monica they decided instead, in the spirit of "Robin Hood," to get the needed gas from cars in Beverly Hills. The "mission" was accomplished through the skill of a young boy whose nickname still remains, fifty years later, "Gas Lips."[12]

The government's restrictions on tires also created numerous games of cat and mouse between those disobeying the regulations and local

An OPA official takes a driver's license number to turn over to the driver's rationing board. The large number of automobiles and nearby skis give testament that not all Angelenos took rationing seriously. (Photograph courtesy of the University of Southern California's Regional History Center).

enforcement authorities." Just like Al Capone in the Prohibition Days," screamed one Los Angeles *Times* headline whose story detailed the operation of a "million-dollar tire bootleg ring." Violators of the tire ordinance were often turned in by service station attendants or neighbors who noticed new tires on a car. Some violators, though, went so far as to have two sets of tires, putting on old tires for daily use and using new ones for long trips out of town. [13]

Problematic for authorities, too, were evasions or abuses of food rationing, particularly meat, sugar, and butter. While consumers with the necessary stamps still faced long lines, some citizens attempted to get around the rationing by serving substitutes they hoped could be passed off as a desired commodity. In one such instance, Los Angeles City Council Member Carl C. Rasmussen attempted to pass horse meat off as steak to six of his dinner guests. According to the councilman, "after they ate the steaks they said they were delicious. They didn't know it was horse meat until I told them." Mayor Bowron, who had skipped the dinner remained a healthy skeptic. According to Rasmussen, "I gave one of the steaks to the Mayor but he said his wife was out of town and he had to feed it to his dog."[14] In Santa Monica, a popular hamburger restaurant that advertised itself as serving the biggest hamburgers in "the West" was shut down by authorities for false advertising after it was discovered that the thickly smothered "hamburgers" were actually thickly disguised horseburgers. As one Los Angeles *Times* writer explained in 1943, "There are Victory Houses, Victory Gardens, Victory Clothing styles, Victory Bonds, Victory Drives, and even Victory Cocktails, but for some reason Victory Meat seems to have missed winning a patriotic accolade."[15]

Despite the trials and tribulations of rationing, the vast majority of the city's population complied with the complicated rules. Given that one in eleven Americans was in uniform at any given time, civilians often felt it was their minimal patriotic duty to sacrifice in the name of the war effort. A common wartime refrain heard throughout the city was "Use it up, wear it out, make it do or do without."

Housing, though, was a difficult commodity to do without. The housing crisis in Los Angeles had become so problematic by 1943 that some unhoused war workers worked night shifts so they would be able to sleep outside in the warmer daylight hours. Newspaper headlines such as, "Pastor Accepts Call Here, But Can't Find Home to Rent" emphasized the shortage. The most famous story of the city's "shelter plight," though, concerned Los Angeles news reporter Chuck Felton, who upon arriving at the scene of a just committed murder, ran past the corpse and on towards the victim's nearby landlady. The reporter still panting from his quick dash pleaded, "Can I rent his apartment?" In response the landlady shook her head and pointing toward a distant figure replied, "Sorry, I already rented it to that police sergeant over there."[16]

The once seemingly open city continued to crowd with the daily arrival of hundreds of war workers and troops. Many of these new arrivals got their first glimpse of sunny Los Angeles stepping off of trains at the city's main railroad terminal, Union Station. Historian John Weaver recalls, "I can still remember the faces of sailors and Marines walking into the winter sunshine at Union Station and just peering at the skies in amazement."[17]

The eleven-million dollar station itself was a sight for wartime residents and troops alike. Often jammed beyond capacity with young troops napping where they could, the station retained a pleasant Southern California feel for its wartime visitors. Orange trees and slightly swaying palm trees shaded its patio areas. Adding to its pleasant feel were the announced arrivals of such romantically named trains as the "Tehachapi, El Capitian, Sunset Limited, Coaster, and the Chief." Station masters, however, were particularly careful not to play nostalgic melodies like "Home Sweet Home" over the station's public address system fearing that such songs would jar the emotions of the young troops. Instead such uplifting songs as "California, Here I Come," were played repeatedly. [18]

Newly arrived troops often took advantage of the station's U.S.O.'s "Troops in Transit" program, which served to help kill hours of "hurry up and wait" G.I. boredom by giving troops tours of nearby Olvera Street and Chinatown. Troops stationed longer in the city also had the opportunity to visit what soon became the world famous, "The Hollywood Canteen." While the Canteen was originally started as a safe G.I. night club it gained early notoriety amongst Angelenos for its wild Halloween Party of 1942. It was at that party that an aspiring radio actress, working as a volunteer hostess, was injured while dancing the latest dance "the jitterbug" (also known as swing dancing). What happened, according to the judge was, "in an extra violent spinning of her body, as a part of the extravagance of this weird dance, she missed connecting with the grasp of her partner, due to his losing balance because a table was pushed against him by the crowd on the sidelines." Thus "the Hollywood Canteen failed in its duty to furnish Miss Edwards with safe employment and permitted a jitterbug enthusiast to indulge in his crazy idea of dancing with plaintiff as a helpless victim." The judge then awarded the actress $8,170 as compensation for her injuries. [19]

A soldier and his girl enjoy a night on the town. (Photograph courtesy of the University of Southern California's Regional History Center).

While the "swinging" Canteen was restricted to G.I.s and its volunteers, residents and service personnel enjoyed the city's night life together at such popular spots as Ciros on Sunset Blvd., the Cocoanut Grove, the Trocadero, the Mocambo, and the Brown Derby. Especially popular for dancing was the Hollywood Palladium which opened its doors in 1940 to a packed crowd of 10,000 and the music of Tommy Dorsey.

For a change of pace, sailors in particular enjoyed the thrill rides provided at the Long Beach Pike. Also popular with those inclined to be near the city's ocean front was dancing at the Aragon Ballroom in Ocean Park. Residents and military alike also were able to enjoy baseball, watching either the Pacific Coast League's Angels at Wrigley Field (42nd and Avalon) or the Hollywood Stars at Gilmore Stadium (now the site of CBS' Television City). Given the war and the loss of available players to the military, the skill level of baseball was substantially diminished. Pitcher Bob Crawford of the Hollywood Stars recalls somewhat humorously that one of his catchers was so pained by hernias that it was a minor miracle each time the player resumed his stance behind the plate. Still the war opened up opportunities for talented aspiring teenage players to play professional baseball. At the tender age of fifteen, Bill Sarni, for example, caught thirty-three games for the Angels in the 1943 season.

One of the more humorous wartime incidents in Los Angeles involved the seldom played Hollywood Star's bullpen catcher Ernie Potocar. During a promotion to increase fan attendance, the Hollywood Stars began a ballot contest that asked fans to vote for their favorite Hollywood Star player. So that fans could follow the voting the stadium's large scoreboard was used to display the daily results. On a whim, several young boys, whose job it was to retrieve the cushions at the end of the game, decided to "stuff" unused ballots they collected on behalf of the practically unknown Potocar. To the great delight of the young boys, and to the disbelief of players and fans alike, slowly, but surely, Potocar's name began its ascension upward. But just as Potocar was about to pass the team's manager, Charlie Root, a very small item appeared the next day in the Los Angeles *Times* sport section. It said Ernie Potocar had been "dealt" to a team in the Arizona-New Mexico League. [20]

For young boys wartime Los Angeles was a particularly exciting place to live. Bruce Fitzpatrick recalls visiting troops whose tents were set up in Exposition Park adjacent to the city's Coliseum. The troops were very friendly, proudly showing the fixated boys their well-maintained rifles. For Fitzpatrick, the highlight of the war would come in June, 1945 when as winner of a scrap metal drive he got to sit near General George Patton at the city's Army-Navy Show. Many youngsters also enjoyed the hobby of plane spotting which entailed correctly identifying any military planes flying overhead. Given Los Angeles' crowded airspace this was no small feat, especially since the spotter was expected to correctly state the exact make and model. In the early months of the war, however, three young boys fishing off a sunken barge a half mile off the Malibu Pier, had a frightening encounter with a group of warplanes. The planes, not seeing the boys, suddenly swooped down and fired on the barge for target practice. Fortunately, the boys were rescued by a nearby coast guard auxiliary boat which had witnessed the attack. [21] Down the coast at Venice Beach, a group of boys swimming watched in amazement the crash landing of a P-38 Interceptor 100 yards off-shore. The pilot, who escaped injury, swam to shore to the delight of the beach crowd. When complemented on his landing skills the pilot replied, "You bet I was lucky. This was the third time."[22]

A group of women aircraft workers enjoying a lunch break at the Vega aircraft plant in Burbank. (Photograph courtesy the National Archives)

Apart from such adventures, the war forced young boys to assume adult roles since many of the community's older males were away in military service. Many boys worked after school in aircraft plants. Women workers there, surrounded by the boys or men too old to be drafted, often related wistfully to one popular wartime song's lament, "They're Either Too Young or Too Old." A common graffiti on plant walls was, "Of all the sad words of tongue or pen, the saddest are these: There are no men." Yet women, like their male counterparts on the front lines, persevered on. Particularly galling, however, were some male attitudes as to how the women war workers should dress. Los Angeles Mayor Fletcher Bowron argued that, "slacks are fine for women in defense factories but good taste and good sense will dictate that they are out of place in City Hall." Bowron angered many of his employees by insisting that all female municipal employees wear only dresses. Bowron added, "Don't let us use the war to undermine these things we like to consider feminine and lady like. I am not old-fashioned, but I don't like to see masculine women much more than feminine traits in men. Let us fight our enemies with all the power and determination we have—but in our own clothes."[23] In response, one young woman complained that in the era of rationing "Why should we women have to give up our silk sox and cut our skirts shorter and you men, who make our laws, still have roomy coats and long trousers." Another woman argued in the spirit of equality that all male employees should be forced to wear kilts. [24]

The growing wartime power of women was instrumental in aiding the city's transformation into America's new "Arsenal of Democracy." Small cabinet shops, for example, were expanded and newly hired women workers there produced ammunition packing cases. A water heater company converted its assembly process into the production of electric generator units. But it was the aircraft industry that created the greatest employment for the city's women. Within the plants they helped to build some of the most important planes of the war including the P-38 Lightning, the B-17 Flying Fortress, the B-25 Mitchell, the SBD Dauntless, and arguably the best fighter plane of the war, the P-51 Mustang. [25] Interestingly, the first Mustang, built by North American Aircraft in Hawthorne, was in the

Complaints of women war workers being inappropriately dressed for war production work led to the wearing of uniforms such as these. (Photograph courtesy of the University of Southern California's Regional History Center.)

Flying over Los Angeles in April 1944 was the then latest version of the North American P-51 Mustang. The newly designed "teardrop" cockpit enclosure allowed the plane's pilots complete vision in all directions. (Photograph courtesy of the University of Southern California's Regional History Center).

air just 100 days after its designers put their pencils to the drawing boards.[26]

So important was aircraft production to the war effort that officials in Long Beach, in July 1942, experimented with "smoke blackouts," a technique in which large white smoke bombs were lit to create a low-lying fog to hide sensitive production areas from a possible air attack.[27] The smoke outs were eventually dropped as air attack fears waned. Nonetheless the city would soon experience its own smoke blackouts by 1943, only this time the culprits were the city's automobiles and the area's massive defense plants.

While war workers and troops protecting the plants worked extremely hard so did members of the cast and crews of the city's movie industry. The war years were especially prolific with most film historians agreeing that the years 1939, 1940, and 1941 represented Hollywood at its zenith. Although the United States was not formally engaged in the war in 1939, it was a year of great tension that saw Nazi Germany "blitzkrieging" its way through Europe. Within the confines of Los Angeles, however, citizens were still talking about the night of December 10, 1938 when the city's skies reddened with the silhouettes of flames and smoke. Many had thought the whole city was aflame and in some ways it was, except it was the city of Atlanta, 1864, and the site of the controlled fire was M.G.M. studios in Culver City, where the movie *Gone With the Wind* was being filmed. [28] Neighbors of the world renowned studio were further "entertained" by the crazy antics of hundreds of little people. Hired to play as "munchkins" for the studio's 1939 *Wizard of Oz* movie, the midgets earned a place in Hollywood lore for their wild takeover of the nearby Culver Hotel.

Given that in 1939 there were more movie theatres (15,115) than banks (14,952), Hollywood in 1939 tried to meet the nation's seemingly insatiable demand by producing such well-known films as Frank Capra's *Mr. Smith Goes to Washington*; John Ford's *Mr. Lincoln, Drums Along the Mohawk*, and *Stagecoach*; and David Selznick's *Gone With the Wind*. 1939 moviegoers could also go to their neighborhood theatres to see such eventual classics as *Wuthering Heights, Ninotchka, Destiny Rides Again, Of Mice and Men, Only Angels Have Wings, Goodbye, Mr. Chips* and *Dark Victory*.

1941 was also a banner year with the release of such great films as *Citizen Kane, How Green Was My Valley, Sergeant York, The Maltese Falcon, Suspicion, The Lady Eve*, and *High Sierra*. However, with the American entrance into the war in December 1941, Hollywood turned its powerful energy into producing such morale boosting films as *Flight Command, Thirty Seconds Over Tokyo*, and *This Is the Army*. But the most enduring classic of the war period remains the 1942 Warner Brother's film, *Casablanca*. Originally written as a Broadway play entitled *Everybody Come's to Rick's*, the script took on added meaning with America's entrance into the war. As script writers continued to rewrite, the cast and crew contended with the incessant noise of warplanes being test flown overhead from the nearby Lockheed plant, while the film took shape as Hollywood's reply to those who once preached isolationism. Even the film's "at all costs neutral" Rick was forced to make a decision on which side in the war he would be. Audiences delighted in his choice and were particularly pleased with the painful but correct sacrifice he made in the still revered airport scene. [29]

Also boosting the city's morale was the February 1942 return of former resident General George S. Patton, Jr. Born in 1885 and raised in the well-to-do suburb of San Marino, Patton had become by April 1941 commander of the Army's 2nd Armored Division. Known somewhat fondly by his troops as "Old Blood and Guts," Patton's zeal for training perfection had made his 2nd Armored division in the words of one Army official, "the toughest, most feared outfit of the whole Army." However, concerned that his troops would not be ready for the rigors of the war's upcoming North African campaign, in February 1942 Patton took a scouting trip to nearby Riverside County, the large desert region located east of Los Angeles. To Patton's great delight, the vast area startlingly resembled the desert areas and heat of North Africa. Satisfied with what he saw, Patton began immediate work on building a tank training center. Within two months of his scouting trip the center was open and operational. [30]

Patton's command of the tank center remains legendary. His rigorous training enabled his ground troops to march eight miles on the desert floor in less than two hours. The troops also became accustomed to subsisting on a canteen of water a day and sleeping in tents that had no heat or electricity. Patton's tank crews were also well prepared being able to perform difficult maneuvers in rapid, deadly accurate fashion.

Patton's Southern California trained troops would play a key role in turning the disastrous North African campaign into the Allies' first major victory. Later in the war Patton's men would be responsible for the successful counterthrust at the Battle of the Bulge. Despite his profane language and flamboyant style, Patton's skill on the battlefield would earn him fame as one of history's great commanders. [31]

Another colorful wartime figure in Los Angeles was renowned radio preacher, Aimee Semple McPherson. Nationally known as "Sister Aimee," her colorful preaching and unorthodox manner attracted scores of G. I. visitors to her large Angelus temple. A superb fund raiser, (one of her popular exhortations at collection time was, "Sister has a headache tonight. Just quiet money please"), McPherson was able to donate thousands of bibles to her military visitors. [32] Although during the war years she was substantially past her prime and popularity, her unexpected death in 1944 brought defiance of rules for wartime tire and gas rationing as over 600 cars bore mourners in her funeral motorcade. [33]

Wartime Los Angeles was also home to young Ellsworth "Sonny" Wisecarver, the infamous "Woo Woo Boy," of World War 2. Wisecarver's worldwide fame began in May of 1944 when he ran off with and married a twenty-one year old mother of two. Sonny's distinction was that he was only 14 years old at the time. As his new wife explained to frenzied reporters, "Age makes no difference. Sonny acts old for 14." She added, "I'm no slick chick. I'm just a girl in love. You take Sinatra and have yourself a swoon. I'll take Sonny."[34] Despite the heartbreak of an annulment and a brief time spent in jail, eighteen months later the "Woo Woo Boy" was back at it again. This time he married a twenty-five year old soldier's wife. Again, the marriage was annulled. Wisecarver, however, was deemed "incorrigible" by a Los Angeles judge and sentenced to a youth camp from which he subsequently escaped. As it could probably only happen in Los Angeles news from the war front was overshadowed by newspaper headlines that blared, "Wisecarver Escapes" and "Wisecarver Still at Large." Perhaps as one Angeleno suggested, the bold headlines were intended to warn local men to get their wives off the streets.[35]

One of the great highlights of Los Angeles' wartime experience was the welcoming home of two of its former residents, American war heroes, General George S. Patton, and Lt. Colonel Jimmy Doolittle. The June

Two former Los Angeles residents, Generals George Patton and Jimmy Doolittle, return for a citywide celebration in their honor in June, 1945. (Photograph courtesy of the University of Southern California's Regional History Center.)

1945 celebration included a flying escort of thirty-six P-40 fighter planes and thirty Liberator Bombers. The two were then saluted with a special Army and Navy war show held in the Coliseum. Through the hard and imaginative work of Hollywood set designers and special effects crews, the Coliseum floor was transformed into a realistic looking war zone. An overflow crowd was then treated to a reenactment of Patton's Third Army's thrust toward Berlin. Patton was especially thrilled with the spectacle. Addressing the crowd, after viewing a simulated tank battle, he stated "What you have just seen is not phantasma but damn near reality and God forgive me, I love that kind of war." The Los Angeles *Times* termed the welcoming parade and war show, "A pageant more spectacular than the city has ever staged for a President, King or Queen...."[36]

Despite much of its eccentric nature, Los Angeles was solidly behind the war effort. Many families and friends suffered the loss of loved ones in the defense of the country. Angelenos also gave generously of themselves in support of such public agencies as the U.S.O. and the Red Cross. Further, their financial generosity, in the form of a Special War Bond campaign, doubled its original goal of $40 million dollars for the building of a new warship. The $80 million raised not only built the heavy cruiser, the U.S.S. *Los Angeles*, but four new destroyers as well. According to historian Roger Lotchin, "In effect, Los Angeles financed a small navy of its own, consisting of five ships, capable of fighting at least a minor naval action, with little or no help from the rest of the country."[37]

Despite disruptions of rationing, blackouts and other forced sacrifices, the Second World War served to unite the people of Los Angeles as never before. In the spirit of patriotism and community spirit, record numbers of Angelenos volunteered themselves serving in such capacities as first aid instructors, air raid wardens, and traffic controllers. While the world war would bring its inevitable long list of local war casualties, the city's sense of shared unity and purpose enabled it to continue as America's new Arsenal of Democracy.

Endnotes

1. William Manchester, *The Glory and the Dream: A Narrative History of America, 1932–1972* (Boston: Little, Brown and Company, 1974), p. 289.
2. Los Angeles *Times*, June 4, 1945.
3. Archie Satterfield, *The Homefront: An Oral History of the War Years in America, 1941–45* (Chicago: Playboy Press, 1981), p. 39.
4. Los Angeles *Times*, May 27, 1942.
5. Richard R. Lingeman, *Don't You Know There's a War On?: The American Home Front, 1941–1945* (New York: G. P. Putnam's Sons, 1970), p. 169.
6. The Tournament of Roses Parade, however, was cancelled. Doris Talbot, a 1942 Rose Parade Princess, recalled that although a sense of normalcy was attempted with a mini Rose Parade at the Huntington Hotel, sadness quickly overcame members of the court as they drove past the empty grandstands on Colorado Boulevard. Los Angeles *Times*, December 27, 1992.
7. Salka Viertel, *The Kindness of Strangers* (New York: Holt, Rinehart and Winston, 1969), p. 239.
8. Carl Zuckmayer, *A Part of Myself: Portrait of an Epoch* (New York: Harcourt, Brace Jonanovich, 1970), p. 352.
9. Los Angeles *Times*, May 22, 1942.
10. Ibid., August 9, 1942.
11. Ibid., May 3, 1944.
12. In the interest of being prudent, the author does not feel it necessary to divulge the identities of those involved in this wartime "indiscretion." Suffice it to say, the author was raised with the story.
13. Los Angeles *Times*, July 5, 1942.
14. Ibid., May 3, 1944.
15. Los Angeles *Times*, Home Magazine, January 3, 1943.
16. Manchester, *The Glory and the Dream*, p. 293.
17. Los Angeles *Times*, September 1, 1989.

18. Ibid., April 19, 1942.
19. Ibid., May 3, 1944.
20. My appreciation to Mr. Bob Moore and Art Verge, Sr. for allowing me to share their story. Mr. Potocar, years later, would remark he was never able to figure out what happened until he was told by a couple of repentant "fans."
21. Los Angeles *Times,* April 27, 1942.
22. Ibid., May 17, 1942.
23. Ibid., April 22, 1942.
24. Ibid., April 23, 1942.
25. Norman Polmar and Thomas B. Allen, *World War 2: America at War, 1941–1945* (New York: Random House, 1991), p. 611.
26. Los Angeles *Times*, May 14, 1942.
27. Ibid., July 21, 1942.
28. Otto Friedrich, *City of Nets: A Portrait of Hollywood in the 1940s* (New York: Harper and Row Publishers, 1986), p. 21.
29. An excellent book on the wartime making of the movie *Casablanca* is Harlan Lebo's, *Casablanca: Behind the Scenes* (New York: Simon and Schuster, 1990).
30. Martin Blumenson, *Patton: The Man Behind the Legend, 1885–1945* (New York: William Morrow and Company, 1985), pp. 160–161.
31. Polmar and Allen, *World War 2,* pp. 620–622.
32. Los Angeles *Times,* December 5, 1942.
33. Lately Thomas, *Storming Heaven: The Lives and Turmoils of Minnie Kennedy and Aimee Semple McPherson* (New York: Morrow Publishing Company, 1970), p. 344.
34. Los Angeles *Times*, May 6, 1944.
35. The wartime story of Sonny Wisecarver is the basis for the popular 1987 movie, *In the Mood.* Available on Lorimar Home Video, the movie stars Patrick Dempsey as Sonny Wisecarver.
36. Los Angeles *Times,* June 10, 1945.
37. Roger Lotchin, *Fortress California, 1910–1961: From Warfare to Welfare* (New York: Oxford University Press, 1992), p. 151.

An Arsenal of Democracy

5

A young, nervous Donald Douglas quietly strode into the room. Across from him was seated the most powerful man in Los Angeles. For Donald Douglas this was it. In desperate need of financial backing this meeting was his last hope of salvaging a life-long dream of building and developing his own planes. At first, the man behind the desk was put off by the youthful appearance of the twenty-eight year old Douglas. But as he listened to Douglas speak, Harry Chandler, publisher of the Los Angeles *Times*, began to take increasing notice of his polite visitor. Chandler understood well the young man's fixation and enthusiasm for aviation. He had it himself. Yet Chandler remained wary of Douglas' request for financial backing. Although it was 1920, aviation was still an embryonic industry full of fiscal risks for investors and physical dangers for participants. Yet the gamble to support Douglas was tempting. It reminded Chandler of the gamble he had taken when he sponsored several of the nation's first air shows ten years earlier. That gamble had paid off. The local air shows had helped to put Los Angeles on the map. They also had attracted to the city such people as the young man standing before him.

Chandler decided to take a calculated gamble. Looking straight at Douglas he remarked, "I don't know whether you know anything about building airplanes but Los Angeles needs more business." Chandler then took out a sheet a paper and began writing the names of nine prominent financial leaders in the city. He then told Douglas, "If each of these men guarantee one-tenth of the loan, I'll guarantee the tenth." Douglas agreed to the offer and then proudly shook Chandler's hand.[1]

Chandler knew that Douglas would have great difficulty in obtaining the other nine signatures. No matter, Chandler had taken a liking to the ambitious and persistent Donald Douglas. Four days later, to Chandler's surprise, Donald Douglas walked into his office, signatures in hand. So began the Douglas Aircraft Company.

Donald Douglas began his new company in late 1920 in the back of a small Santa Monica barbershop. By 1939, his planes were world renowned and admired for their reliability and sleek design. Donald Douglas had come a long way. Arriving in Los Angeles in 1915, the recent M.I.T. graduate had gone straight to work for the man who had lured him west with a job offer, the experimental plane builder, Glen Martin. The timing proved prophetic for both men as orders for their planes surged with the spread of the First World War throughout Europe. In working alongside Martin, Douglas learned a valuable lesson—government contracts were invaluable, for their orders were large and the government usually paid its bill.

Yet when Donald Douglas began his new company he did not want it to be solely dependent on military orders. Thus, despite the onset of the Great Depression, Douglas continued to expand his company's operations to include the large-scale production of civilian aircraft. In 1932, the first of the DC (Douglas Commercial) models took to the air. The polished, all metal, twin engine DC-1 was an instant hit with the American public. Douglas quickly followed with the slightly modified DC-2. Its shiny, sleek look earned the affection of child-star Shirley Temple who sang its praises in the popular song, "The Good Ship Lollipop." The DC-2 was followed in 1935 by what most aviation experts now consider to be the prototype of today's modern passenger aircraft, the DC-3. Responsible for introducing hundreds of thousands of Americans to flying, the DC-3 would also gain

Donald Douglas (far left) meets with a group of impressed War Department officials to discuss the building of military aircraft. (Photograph courtesy of the University of Southern California's Regional History Center).

fame in World War 2 as the C-47. Affectionately known by troops as the "Gooney Bird," this military transport plane was cited by Gen. Dwight Eisenhower as one of the four key weapons responsible for helping to win the war (the others being the Bazooka, the Jeep, and the Atomic Bomb). Proving their durability, in 1993 more than one thousand DC-3's were still flying as either cargo or passenger aircraft.

The exceptional dependability and safety record of the early DCs fostered the public's trust in a still youthful aviation industry. By 1939, the now world renowned Douglas Aircraft Company had not only survived the Great Depression but had expanded its operations to include the employment of more than 7,000 workers. While the company continued to mass produce the popular DCs, the outbreak of war in Europe in the same year brought forth a cascade of military plane orders. Donald Douglas was then faced with a crucial business decision. Should he retool and expand his plant operations to take advantage of the large military orders or should he save expenditures and continue to emphasize his already successful civilian aircraft line. For better or worse, the decision was made for him as the conflagration of the war quickly spread to threaten the national security interests of the United States. Subsequent American military involvement forced the Douglas Aircraft Company to work and expand at break neck speeds. Allied war production needs also added demands on Douglas and his company. When war broke out in Europe on September 1, 1939 the company employed 7,589 workers. By 1944, Douglas Aircraft had expanded to six major production plants employing more than 160,000 workers.

During the war, 29,385 planes came off the Douglas assembly line. This remarkable figure constitutes, by weight, a full 14 percent of all aircraft produced by the United States in the Second World War.

During the nation's defense build-up, privately owned companies, such as Douglas Aircraft, were able to expand their operations assisted by federal investment dollars. One federal agency that played a key role in governing these investments was the Reconstruction Finance Corporation (RFC). Given the need for rapid wartime response, and the blessing of cheap available land, the RFC encouraged the expansion of existing facilities over the construction of new ones. Through its subsidiary, the Defense Plant Corporation (DPC), it oversaw the expenditure in Los Angeles of more than 312 million dollars in plant expansion efforts between 1939 and 1944. The DPC also spent 142 million dollars on the construction of new plants. In all, more than 1,000 plants were expanded in Los Angeles County during the war years. During the height of the war, from 1942 to 1944, 479 new defense plants were added to the region's manufacturing base.[2]

Two other important subsidiaries of the Reconstruction Finance Corporation were the Rubber Reserve Corporation and the Metals Reserve Corporation. The Rubber Reserve Corporation was formed in 1942 after Japanese military conquests gave Japan control of most of the world's natural rubber supply. To meet wartime demands, the Rubber Reserve Corporation began large-scale production efforts aimed at turning out eight hundred thousand tons of synthetic rubber a year. During the war, Los Angeles' ability to provide oil, an essential raw material in the production of synthetic rubber, led it to become the west coast's leading manufacturer of the product.[3] Los Angeles defense officials also had substantial contact with the Metals Reserve Corporation, the federal government's leading procurer of essential metals. The services of this RFC subsidiary were especially vital to Los Angeles' plane manufacturers and shipbuilders.[4]

The beneficiaries of this massive wartime investment capital ranged from the already large aircraft manufacturers to small manufacturing concerns. The Defense Plant Corporation was responsible for supplying the capital for 71 percent of the aircraft factories, 58 percent of the aluminum plants and 96 percent of new rubber plants for the western region of the United States. Further, it was responsible for financing fourteen of the fifteen largest aircraft plants built during the Second World War.[5]

The region's proximity to the Pacific war and its growing industrial capacity attracted not only defense dollars but workers as well. Between April 1940 and April 1944, an estimated 780,000 persons migrated into the Los Angeles area. Nearly 80 percent of these immigrants were under the age of 45, and they were responsible for increasing Los Angeles' wartime labor supply by 25 percent.[6] To further expand their wartime labor supply, Los Angeles industry leaders began offering employment opportunities to groups previously neglected. Among the first hired were local white males that were retired, handicapped, or still school-aged. Although this helped to offset the initial loss of personnel to the draft, the tremendous production increases demanded by the war forced the further opening of employment doors to women and minorities. Yet, despite the obvious and desperate need for workers, the resistance to hiring women was widespread throughout the defense industries. Several plant operators in the early months of the war claimed that females would prove inept at war production work. Several others argued that women on the assembly line would distract male workers from the work at hand. There was also large-scale resistance to women workers from males in the work force. With the Depression still fresh in their minds, many males perceived women workers as future threats to fair wages and job security.[7]

While discrimination against women workers remained strong throughout the war, the hiring of females by defense industries increased as women proved themselves capable of heavy war work. So impressed were several aircraft companies that they initiated recruiting campaigns to get more women workers. Lockheed Aircraft, for example, instituted a "Victory Visitors" program which sent married women employees door to door in local neighborhoods to recruit full-time housewives for part-time defense production work.[8] Several companies attempted to bring the work to local women by setting up small assembly plants adjacent to residential neighborhoods. Overall, these innovative methods helped to add thousands of desperately needed defense workers to the labor force. So dramatic was the change that the number of women employees in the six Southern California aircraft plants went from 143 in 1941 to nearly 65,000 by the summer of 1943.[9]

With their lunch pails open for inspection, so as to prevent theft from factory floors, a group of women war workers happily leaves a war plant after a hard day's work. (Photograph courtesy of the University of Southern California's Regional History Center.)

In sharp contrast to the Depression years, the thousands of new female arrivals to Los Angeles during the war found themselves in the unusual position of being able to chose from a wide variety of jobs. Typical of the thousands of young women who came to Los Angeles in search of high paying defense work, Juanita Loveless arrived in Los Angeles with just the clothes on her back and a few dollars in her pocket. Her fortunes changed quickly. Working at a local gas station she recalled that, "everyday someone came in saying, 'Do you want a job?' My head was going crazy. They were recruiting for any kind of work you wanted. Newspapers just splashed everywhere: 'Help Wanted,' 'Help Wanted,' 'Jobs,' 'Jobs,' 'Jobs.'" There was also "Propaganda on every radio station: 'If you're an American citizen, come to gate so and so'—at Lockheed or at the shipyards in San Pedro.... You were bombarded."[10]

Los Angeles, however, despite gaining substantially in its labor supply by employing women, still faced large shortages of workers in 1943 and late into 1944. Part of the problem was rapid industrial expansion, where the number of new job openings often outstripped the number of workers entering the labor force. Employees accepted this problem and combatted it through wide-scale recruiting. High job turnover, however, was unacceptable to defense producers. Job turnover contributed to shortages of workers because valuable employees were needed to recruit, process and train new workers. Despite calls that leaving one's job for anything but military service was unpatriotic, high job-turnover rates nonetheless plagued the defense industries. During the first six months of 1943, for example, aircraft plants along the Pacific Coast hired 150,000 and lost 138,000 through labor turnover.[11] Organized labor blamed the high turnover rates on low wages while management accused those quitting of lacking patriotism. Despite the dispute, both groups agreed something needed to be done and together they sought the means to stem the flow of high worker turnover.[12]

Especially problematic were the large numbers of women involved in job turnover. The causes were multifold. Many women entering the work force for the very first time found factory work unappealing and often left it for employment in service sector work. Others, quite understandably, found juggling a full-time job, while raising children and maintaining a home, to be too difficult. Still others cited the lack of adequate child care as the cause for their leaving defense work.

The continual loss of these women workers forced the defense industry to completely rethink its employment practices. Several Los Angeles aircraft plants responded to the worker hemorrhage by redesigning their assembly lines to include such back-saving devices as chain hoists and load lifts. Also involved in the factory floor renovation was the inclusion of large conveyor belts, streamlined tools, and worker rest stations.[13]

Defense employers also looked outside the factory gates to find problems linked to possible worker turnover. Workers' complaints of being greeted with closed stores and banks when their long shifts let out, led several companies to make arrangements with stores and banks to keep extended business hours. Yet, the most difficult complaint to address, and the one most often cited by women workers, was the lack of adequate child care. So pressing was the problem that the aircraft industry as a whole began lobbying for federal action. Arguing that the continuing loss of women workers would curtail defense production, Congress responded to employers' pleas with the 1942 passage of the Lanham Act.[14] This act, which provided federal funding for an extensive array of on-site child care centers, reduced significantly the loss of women day-shift workers. However, the program was completely ineffectual in curtailing the loss of night and graveyard shift workers because the on-site child care program was available to mothers only during daytime hours.[15]

Also contributing to the problems of high wartime-employee turnover was the pirating of laborers, a practice particularly widespread in the shipbuilding industry during the years 1940–1942. In the shipyards the need for experienced ship builders forced many companies into bidding wars over skilled employees. Substantial numbers of these skilled workers were "pirated" away to competing yards with offers of better wages and working conditions. Also hard hit in the bidding war were the aircraft industry and the Pacific Electric Railway which suffered substantial losses of workers to the higher-paying shipbuilding industry.[16] On a larger scale, the extensive growth of shipbuilding along the Pacific Coast prompted fears that the local labor supply would be "raided" by outside maritime yards and their subcontractors.[17]

As worker turnover continued to mount, with many war plants suffering over 100 percent turnover a year, the War Manpower Commission (WMC) in January 1943 began enforcement of an employment stabilization program in Southern California. The program, drawn up by local representatives of both labor and management acting as the Southern California Area Manpower Committee, was voluntary in nature.[18] The plan provided that no worker would be hired in any predetermined "essential industry" without a certificate of availability. To obtain a certificate, the worker had to apply and receive approval from the current employer or from a representative of the War Manpower Commission.

Under the WMC guidelines, employers could retain workers whom they felt essential to their production, although the employee could appeal for a release through the Commission.[19] The intent of the employment stabilization plan, which went into effect on January 18, 1943, was to insure that a worker would only be hired when the change of employment was determined to be in the best interests of the war effort. The program, which was in effect throughout Southern California, began first in twenty-nine major industries including aircraft production, shipbuilding, food processing, and transportation.[20]

Another related program, initiated in 1943, was the wage stabilization plan. Protracted negotiations between labor and management over a wage schedule made the program difficult to establish. In spite of numerous complications, both the shipbuilding and aircraft industries instituted wage stabilization plans for their industries by the summer of 1943.[21]

Although the stabilization plans were effective in reducing turnover in the industries that used them, the growing shortages of workers in Los Angeles created further problems for defense contracters. To maintain production levels defense firms in Los Angeles County averaged a 45-hour work week throughout the early months of 1943.[22] A 48-hour or longer work week was common, however, by August 1943 when the federal government made wage stabilization mandatory for all firms employing eight or more people (unless the industry was specifically exempted).[23] While the extra hours aided production efforts, defense producers were soon hampered by increased absenteeism. To obtain an average of 48 work hours a week, many companies found it necessary to operate under a schedule that exceeded 50 hours a week.[24]

Much of the absenteeism was not related to a lack of patriotism or laziness; rather it was due to workers trying to do too much. Hubert R. Harnish, Area Director for the Southern California War Manpower Commission, concluded that the 48-hour work week would not really make a difference, arguing that "If they are working the regular 40 hours," people "are working somewhere else as a rule."[25] Further, the generally higher rates of absenteeism among women is explained, in part, by the significant numbers of working mothers. Even women without children found the arduous work difficult to do day in and day out.

Some industry officials, such as the personnel director of the California Shipbuilding Corporation, Los Angeles' largest wartime shipyard, minimized the need for more than one eight-hour shift off a week. Referring to women workers at the Calship yard, the official stated: "Here we are on 7-day operation, so that at least 6 out of the 7 weeks women have a day off during the week so that they can take care of whatever they have to take care of rather than be off every Sunday."[26] However, for the thousands of working mothers, "to take care of whatever they have to care of," often meant nursing a sick child, grocery shopping, doing the laundry, house cleaning, etc.

Absenteeism among men often involved repeat offenders. Habitual absenteeism was combated by company threats to notify draft boards of the employee's upcoming availability. Several companies resorted to paying employees on Mondays to increase attendance and reduce weekend drinking sprees.

Still the problem of absenteeism proved to be a minor one overall. The key issue for Los Angeles defense industries was meeting the shortages of workers. Through the War Manpower Commission, over one-and-a-half million job placements were handled during its first year of operation.[27] With the weight of the federal government behind it, the War Manpower Commission met with great success in recruiting nationwide.

The changes brought by war proved indelible to both workers and local industry. In spite of numerous problems related to retaining workers and maintaining production schedules, the defense industries of Los Angeles succeeded in producing vast quantities of much needed defense materials. An examination of the effects of rapid industrialization, implementation of new technologies, and the vast infusion of government capital in several of Los Angeles' major defense industries provides a good assessment of the war's dramatic impact on the region's industrial development.

Perhaps no other Los Angeles industry was impacted as much from the war as the area's shipbuilding industry. Before the summer of 1941 the shipbuilding industry of Los Angeles was relatively small, employing an average of 1,000 employees in 1939.[28] Until 1940, twenty years had past since a large ship had been constructed in the yards. Although government contracts for large ships filtered into the industry in 1940, Los Angeles shipyards continued to be characterized by scattered launchings through 1941.

As in aircraft production the continual and growing infusion of government shipbuilding contracts after 1940 completely transformed the small industry. Starting in the middle of 1941 employment in the shipyards took tremendous leaps as contractors raced to expand their yards and to begin work on the ships they had been hired to build. Shipyard employment soared to 22,000 in October 1941. By late December 1941 shipbuilding had become the second largest manufacturing industry in the Los Angeles area.[29]

The rapid expansion of the area's shipbuilding industry was not without its problems. Given the industry's two decade lapse in constructing large ships, numerous fundamental changes were necessary before construction could proceed at a rapid pace. One key problem of the Los Angeles shipbuilding industry was attracting and retaining of skilled shipyard workers. Due to the industry's relatively small size prior to the war, the numbers of experienced workers was quite limited. Thus, these workers became quite valuable to the shipyards; they were hired not only for their skills and experience in shipbuilding, but also for the information they could impart to inexperienced workers. As defense orders flowed into the industry, the services of these workers became a source of competition among shipyards. Experienced shipyard workers often found themselves in the midst of recruiting and bidding wars. The Roosevelt administration responded to the nationwide problem in late 1940 by forming the Shipbuilding Stabilization Committee. Comprised of representatives from both management and labor, the committee sought to prevent the pirating of labor that had plagued the shipbuilding industry during the First World War. The committee divided the country into four zones with the objective of reaching a basic agreement between management and labor on work rules and wage scales in each zone. Under this division Los Angeles fell into the Pacific Coast zone. As the shipbuilding industry literally blossomed overnight, the work of the committee to establish uniform wage scales throughout the yards took on increasing importance.[30]

Competition for shipyard workers also took place between the AFL and the CIO unions. Although Los Angeles had historically been known as an "open shop" city, the area's shipyards had become predominantly union since the mid-1930s.[31] While the AFL was the dominant labor organizer in the Los Angeles shipyards, the CIO did make some inroads. Fighting what they perceived as "back-door" agreements between large shipyards and the AFL, the CIO continually turned to federal authorities to prevent the AFL's complete dominance of the industry. The AFL in turn accused the CIO of "unpatriotic activities," charging that the CIO raided AFL locals for new members. Subsequent federal intervention in local shipyard labor disputes significantly reduced problems of "pirating" and labor union squabbling.[32]

The sudden upsurge of shipbuilding in Los Angeles created numerous production problems within the industry itself. Among them was the widespread lack of equipment. In the early days of the defense buildup a shortage of welding machines was blamed for holding up the production of much needed ships. By the time the needed welding machines arrived, however, war had broken out and the shipyards did not have enough workers to operate them.[33]

Los Angeles shipyards also had to contend with "bottleneck" problems caused by shortages of materials and inadequate transportation systems. The California Shipbuilding Corporation's report in "Production in Shipbuilding Plants," pointed out that a train carload of materials from the east, which in 1942 would have taken 10 to 12 days to arrive, by 1943, required 20 to 21 days to make the trip because of heavy congestion on the nation's railways. This was a major problem since an estimated 75 percent of the shipbuilding materials prior to 1944 came from the east by rail to Los Angeles.[34]

The city's shipbuilders attempted to countermand the "bottleneck" problems by seeking federal funds to develop industries that could produce the materials they needed. Their efforts were led by Henry J. Kaiser who, among his many industrial activities, was the majority owner of California

Los Angeles' crowded Calship shipyard was the site of the building of a then world record 15 Liberty ships in June 1942. (Photograph courtesy of the National Archives)

Shipbuilding Corporation. In trying to reduce bottlenecks plaguing West Coast defense industries, Kaiser also sought to end the virtual lock of eastern industrialists on the manufacture of finished steel products by developing a steel manufacturing facility in the west. Kaiser's efforts received the tacit support of President Franklin D. Roosevelt on the grounds that dispersal of the steel industry would make it less vulnerable to enemy attack. Further, Roosevelt wanted to see an end to the monopolistic practices used by eastern steel industrialists. In 1942, Kaiser was issued a 150 million dollar Reconstruction Finance Corporation loan to build a new steel manufacturing plant.[35]

Kaiser located the steel plant in Fontana, which was estimated to be just out of the range of Japanese attack planes but within easy train distance of the Los Angeles harbor shipyards. The Fontana steel plant, which began full-scale operations in August 1943, produced heavy steel plates and structural members necessary for large-scale ship building. Federal loans had also been used to enlarge local machine shops and foundries. Turning from the production of such light metal items as wire and tin plate, local manufacturers soon produced metal parts for boilers, engines, pumps, and winches. This expansion, made local shipbuilders less reliant on eastern manufacturing and reduced bottleneck problems in their yards.[36]

With federal financial assistance, a large work force, and a rapidly adaptable manufacturing base, Los Angeles shipbuilders proceeded to deliver hundreds of ships during the war. This was especially remarkable given the locality's weak shipbuilding industry prior to the war. Henry J. Kaiser played a prominent role in the area's shipbuilding success. In 1940, Kaiser and his associates, backed by the Maritime Commission, organized from scratch the California Shipbuilding Corporation. Known as Calship, the yard was located on 175 acres of semi-tidelands on Los Angeles' Terminal Island. Beginning production of Liberty ships in May 1941, the yard, thirteen months later, broke the existing world's record for ship production by delivering 15 Liberty ships in June 1942.[37] By standardizing the design and specifications for all its government ordered ships, Calship was able to launch 111 ships in 1942, more than any other yard in the United States.[38] Ship production at Calship was further speeded with the completion of Henry Kaiser's Fontana steel plant in August 1943. As a result, Calship was the country's second largest emergency shipyard, launching 467 ships between September 27, 1941 and September 27, 1945.[39]

Los Angeles was also the home of several other major shipyards. Consolidated Steel Corporation delivered more than 500 vessels, while the Bethlehem Shipbuilding Corporation repaired and returned to service an average of two large naval vessels for every work day during the war. Todd Shipyards took over the previously failed Los Angeles Shipbuilding and Drydock Company and converted 2,376 ships during the last three years of the war.[40]

During the war the shipyards of Los Angeles handled more than one and one-half billion dollars in shipbuilding contracts.[41] At the war's peak they employed some 90,000 employees, including 55,000 at Calship.[42]

The rapid rise of Los Angeles' shipbuilding industry from 1939 to 1945 gives testimony to the region's adaptability for wartime industrial growth. However, the greatest beneficiary of this adaptability was the aircraft industry. In the short space of five years the aircraft industry in Los Angeles had expanded so rapidly that its percentage of local workers

Several hundred engineers are hard at work in this specially designed drafting room at Lockheed Aircraft in Burbank. The room's revolutionary design allowed engineers to quickly move between planning and drafting areas with minimum disturbance to others. (Photograph courtesy of the University of Southern California's Regional History Center).

soared from five percent in 1937 to more than forty percent during its wartime peak.[43] By 1944, the aircraft industry led Los Angeles' second largest industry, shipbuilding, by a six-to-one ratio in payroll and employee figures.[44] Its development affected the region as no other wartime industry and, unlike the shipbuilding industry, its impact was longstanding.

As the dominant force in wartime Los Angeles, the aircraft industry played a prominent role in shaping the local economy. At its wartime high, the industry employed 228,400 workers.[45] These substantial numbers of employees, many of whom had families, helped to continue the economic growth of service-related industries during the war. Much of the financing of the large payrolls came from defense orders. The United States government by June of 1945 had placed more than 7 billion dollars worth of aircraft orders.[46] The financial impact on Los Angeles was nothing short of phenomenal. For small manufacturers' the plane orders were a "boon" as they quickly expanded their operations to meet the subcontract demands of an already overwhelmed aircraft industry. By 1944, an estimated 4,000 separate "war plants" were located in Los Angeles with the large majority involved in aircraft manufacturing.[47]

The aircraft industry's success in Los Angeles, like the shipbuilding industry's, can be traced to its ability to expand rapidly. While its foundation was developed for commercial aviation, early financing for its large growth came from foreign defense orders. America's defense build-up in 1940 and subsequent orders further encouraged expansion. Aircraft manufacturers, however, remained wary that overexpansion would doom the profitable industry if orders declined. The attack on Pearl Harbor proved to be the turning point. Government financing of expansion and large backlogs of orders encouraged the industry's growth. Aircraft manufacturers themselves adapted and worked together to meet production needs. In early 1942, the chief executive officers of Southern California aircraft companies formed the Aircraft War Production Council (AWPC). The council sought to increase aircraft production by unifying the industry. In a unique departure from the characteristically competitive market, the Southern California aircraft manufacturers shared patents, facilities, and even personnel to meet production schedules. The program was so successful that a year after formation of the AWPC, eastern aircraft manufacturers joined the group, which then became known as the National Aircraft War Production Council, Inc (NAWPC).[48]

The unified effort saved millions of production hours. Among the major successes of NAWPC was the sharing of trade secrets such as

Sunny Los Angeles proved especially advantageous to aircraft manufacturers giving them extra space outside to assemble their planes. Lockheed workers here are completing work on a group of P-38 Lightnings. (Photograph courtesy of the University of Southern California's Regional History Center).

Douglas Aircraft's flush riveting technique, which in turn revolutionized the manufacturing of aircraft. The council's implementation of standardized designs and parts further aided productivity. The assistance of the federal government in directing and redirecting materials to the plants that needed them also aided the building of the war planes. The workers themselves, increasingly gaining experience, saw their own productivity rise. The average worker's productivity increased from 23 to 70 pounds of aircraft between 1941 and 1943. As a result of these gains Los Angeles aircraft production in 1943 increased 100 percent over 1942, and in 1944 rose another 50 percent before declining.[49]

Bringing the war to the enemy is this B-17F bomber which has just successfully struck a German aircraft plant. Although the B-17 was designed and primarily built by Boeing, both Los Angeles-based Douglas Aircraft and Lockheed Aircraft also built the deadly effective bomber. (Photograph courtesy of the National Archives)

Beyond the phenomenal production statistics of Los Angeles' aircraft factories were the exploits of the planes themselves. The people of Los Angeles were undoubtedly proud of their planes such as Lockheed's P-38 Lightning, called the "fork-tailed devil" by the Luftwaffe, and North American's B-25 Mitchell, the plane used in Lt. Colonel's Jimmy Doolittle's morale boosting bombing raid on Japan in April 1942.[50] The success of these planes and the many others being turned out by the six major aircraft producers in Los Angeles earned worldwide admiration.

The growing stature of Los Angeles' aircraft industry was earned through the hard work and sacrifices of thousands of workers. Many who worked building the vast numbers of planes that would help change the course of the war, had never entered an industrial facility prior to their employment. The experience was particularly profound for women and minorities. Previously excluded on a large-scale from the industrial work force, their subsequent wartime participation proved to be the backbone of the aircraft industry's expansion. African-Americans, for example, accounted for three to seven percent of the work forces at various aircraft plants.[51] And at the peak of worker shortages, women comprised 42 percent of the industry's total work force. In fact, in several companies their numbers made up over 50 percent of the work force.[52] Thus, the large-scale incorporation of women in the industrial work force proved to be the single greatest factor in easing the war's severe "manpower" shortage.

During the war period both the AFL and the CIO made significant gains in Los Angeles' aircraft plants. Although the rivalry between the two unions continued, both fought management on a variety of issues. Further, both did so while maintaining no-strike pledges with management. The key issues addressed by both unions were worker-oriented concerns, such as higher wages, seniority rights, and handling of employee grievances. By maintaining staunch support behind the war effort and seeking reasonable resolutions to employee concerns, both labor unions made substantial gains in membership.

The ability of the unions to garner mainstream support from aircraft workers was by far their greatest accomplishment. This permitted the unions to defeat a 1944 anti-union bid proposed by the Los Angeles Merchants and Manufacturing Association.

The renewed effort to end unions in Los Angeles, which prior to the war had the backing of the major aircraft manufacturers, now fell flat from lack of support throughout the defense industries. The change of heart was led by the aircraft industry's fear of alienating its large number of union employees. Similar to many other Los Angeles defense producers, the aircraft industry was willing to share its bountiful wartime harvest with labor in return for worker productivity.[53]

The labor movement throughout Los Angeles during the war was characterized by very few strikes. When "job actions" or strikes did occur, most lasted one day or less. The relative success of the labor-management relationship during this period is in large part due to the federal government. As holder of the purse strings for industrial expansion and investment, it often could successfully intervene in labor-management conflict. Further, through its auspices it set up programs, such as wage stabilization, that encouraged improved working relationships between labor and management.[54]

Overall production in Los Angeles was also facilitated by the involvement of the federal government. Through its financial backing, the industries of Los Angeles obtained record growth levels. Among key changes were the development of local material producing industries such as steel and aluminum, a major expansion of plant facilities, a large, well-trained labor force, and the accumulation of substantial amounts of venture capital.[55]

Los Angeles proved to be a worthy investment for the federal government. The region's defense industries responded to the monumental task of supporting a two-front war by producing a wide range of such vitally needed defense goods as ships, tanks, guns, uniforms, and parachutes. Further, Los Angeles aircraft manufacturers', whose planes were the backbone of the Allied war effort, produced an astounding one new war plane every seven minutes. Emerging from the war as the nation's second largest defense producer, Los Angeles had earned a worldwide reputation as a leader in innovation, industrial prowess and technological development. For the American people, especially those in search of employment and a way to demonstrate their patriotism on the homefront, wartime Los Angeles had become the nation's new industrial Mecca.

Endnotes

1. Wayne Biddie, *Barons of the Sky: From Early Flight to Strategic Warfare—The Story of the American Aerospace Industry* (New York: Simon and Schuster Publishing, 1991), p. 132.
2. Security-First National Bank, *Monthly Summary,* January 1945. Created by Congress in August 1940, the DPC became the largest investor in the defense industries of Los Angeles. Within the first two years of its existence, the agency invested nearly a third of a billion dollars constructing not only aircraft plants, but shipyards, aluminum plants, steel mills and other industrial facilities throughout Southern California as well.
3. Marvin Brienes, "Smog Comes to Los Angeles," *Southern California Quarterly* 58:4 (1976), p. 518.
4. Nash, *The American West Transformed.*
5. Ibid., p. 19.
6. U.S. Bureau of the Census, "Wartime Changes in Population and Family Characteristics, Los Angeles Congested Production Area: April 1944," Series CA-2, No.5, pp. 1–3.
7. James Richard Wilburn, "Social and Economic Aspects of the Aircraft Industry in Metropolitan Los Angeles During World War II," (Ph.D. dissertation, University of California, Los Angeles, 1971), p. 203.
8. Sherna Berger Gluck, *Rosie the Riveter Revisited: Women, The War, and Social Change* (Boston: Twayne Publishers, 1987), pp. 12–13.
9. Ibid., pp. 203–204.
10. Ibid., p. 135.
11. 78th Congress, first sess., House, Subcommittee of Committee of Naval Affairs, *Hearings on Congested Areas,* Part 8, p. 2032 (8 parts, Washington, 1944), hereafter cited as *Congested Area Hearings.*
12. Wilburn, "The Aircraft Industry in Metropolitan Los Angeles During World War II," p. 85.
13. Carleton Champe, "Women Only," North American *Skyline,* (May June 1944, Vol. 5, No. 2), pp. 10–11.

14. Karen Anderson, *Wartime Women: Sex Roles, Family Relations, and the Status of Women During World War II* (Westport: Greenwood Press, 1981), p. 125; D'Ann Campbell, *Women at War with America: Private Lives in a Patriotic Era* (Cambridge: Harvard University Press, 1984), pp. 13–14.

15. *Congested Area Hearings,* Part 8, pp. 1794, 2036.

16. Wilburn, "The Aircraft Industry in Metropolitan Los Angeles During World War II," p. 103.

17. 78th Congress, first sess., House, Committee on the Merchant Marine and Fisheries, *Production in Shipbuilding Plants,* Part 2, p. 169 (4 parts, Washington, 1943), hereafter cited as *Production in Shipbuilding Plants.*

18. Security-First National Bank, *Monthly Summary,* February 1943.

19. Wilburn, "The Aircraft Industry in Metropolitan Los Angeles During World War II," p. 103.

20. Security-First National Bank, *Monthly Summary,* February, 1943. *Congested Area Hearings,* Part 8, pp. 1988–1989.

21. Wilburn, "The Aircraft Industry in Metropolitan Los Angeles During World War II," pp. 148–149; *Production in Shipbuilding Plants,* Part 1, pp. 122–124.

22. Security-First National Bank, *Monthly Summary,* March 1943.

23. Ibid., November 1943.

24. Ibid., March 1943.

25. *Production in Shipbuilding Plants,* Part 2, p. 168.

26. Ibid., Part 2, p. 260.

27. Wilburn, "The Aircraft Industry in Metropolitan Los Angeles During World War II," p. 105.

28. Arthur G. Coons and Arjay R. Miller. *An Economic and Industrial Survey of Los Angeles and San Diego Areas* (Sacramento: California State Planning Board, 1941), p. 198.

29. Security-First National Bank, *Monthly Summary,* February 1943. 30. *Production in Shipbuildinq Plants,* Part 1, p. 2.

31. Ibid., Part 2, p. 290.

32. Ibid., Part 2, pp. 256–257.

33. Ibid., Part 2, p. 175.

34. Ibid., Part 2, pp. 204–205; 268–271; 281.

35. Nash, *The American West Transformed,* pp. 27–28.

36. Clifford M. Zierer, ed., *California and the Southwest* (New York: John Wiley and Sons, 1956), pp. 307–308.

37. Charles F. Queenan, *The Port of Los Angeles: From Wilderness to World Port* (Los Angeles: Los Angeles Harbor Department, 1982), p. 87.

38. Security-First National Bank, *Monthly Summary,* February 1943.

39. Queenan, *The Port of Los Angeles,* p. 87. City of Los Angeles, Board of Harbor Commissioners, *Annual Report: For the Fiscal Year Beginning July 1, 1946, and Ending June 30, 1947.*

40. Queenan, *Port of Los Angeles,* p. 91.

41. City of Los Angeles, Board of Harbor Commissioners, *Annual Report 1946–1947.*

42. Queenan, *Port of Los Angeles,* p. 91.

43. Coons and Miller, *An Economic and Industrial Survey,* p. 184.

44. Wilburn, "The Aircraft Industry in Metropolitan Los Angeles During World War II," p. 68.

45. Ibid., p. 47.

46. Nash, *The American West Transformed,* p. 26.

47. Wilburn, "The Aircraft Industry in Metropolitan Los Angeles During World War II," pp. 54–55.

48. Ibid., pp. 27–29.

49. Ibid., pp. 45–50.

50. Bill Gunston, *Aircraft of World War II* (New York: Crescent Books, 1980), pp. 133, 163. 51. Ibid., p. 248.

52. Wilburn, "The Aircraft Industry in Metropolitan Los Angeles During World War II," pp. 236–237.

53. Ibid., p. 153.

54. For a thorough discussion on the role of organized labor in Los Angeles during the Second World War, see Gene Tipton, "The Labor Movement in the Los Angeles Area During the Nineteen Forties," (Ph.D. dissertation, University of California, Los Angeles, 1953), pp. 110–147; Wilburn, "The Aircraft Industry in Metropolitan Los Angeles During World War II," pp. 114-161.

55. Security-First National Bank, *Monthly Summary,* June 1943.

The Perils of Rapid Wartime Growth

6

To Los Angeles, like many other industrial areas of the United States, the Second World War brought both prosperity and adversity. On the positive side, the massive influx of government war contracts helped to fuel record economic growth for the region. However, the rapid wartime development of Los Angeles also generated large-scale problems involving inadequate housing, congested public transportation, and an overburdened health care system.

By the spring of 1942, Congress had become increasingly concerned that growing labor and urban problems in the nation's industrial centers were responsible for lagging defense production quotas. Alarmed by these developments, the House Naval Affairs Committee in late 1942 appointed a subcommittee to investigate congested production areas in the United States. The "Subcommittee on Congested Areas," whose members represented a cross section of all the important war production areas of the United States, focused its attention primarily on the problems of the newly developing manufacturing and assembly centers in the west. Its investigation in the spring and fall of 1943 included the west coast cities of San Diego, Los Angeles, San Francisco, Portland and Seattle.[1]

The subcommittee's study concluded that the newly industrialized areas of the west were hard pressed to meet the demands of the nation's rapid defense mobilization. Of particular concern was the negative impact that the massive migration of defense workers was having on local governments. Indeed, the dramatically increased demands on such public resources as schools and water and sewer systems, was forcing the near bankruptcy of several west coast cities. The subcommittee's report also noted that Los Angeles proved to be "by far the most challenging" and "in many ways the most perplexing" of the west coast production areas investigated.[2] Subcommittee members who visited and studied the area from November 7 to November 15, 1943 were particularly struck by the lack of federal recognition of Los Angeles' war-related problems and the city's importance to the war effort. Although Los Angeles was the nation's leading aircraft producer and one of the country's leading shipbuilders, the city had not been assigned a representative to the President's Executive Committee for Congested Production Areas.[3] Further, through its hearings, the subcommittee discovered that many within the federal government still perceived Los Angeles as simply a "branch-plant town."

Chief among Los Angeles war-related problems was the increasing lack of available housing for newly arriving defense workers. Ironically, prior to 1942, Los Angeles had a substantial surplus of available housing. Blessed with a decentralized base, large open spaces, and a history as a migratory center, prewar Los Angeles was able to handle large numbers of new arrivals. In 1940, the Bureau of the Census estimated that Los Angeles County had a vacancy supply of nearly 68,000 family dwelling units. The number remained stable with the development of new suburban cities outside the central city's core. Among the new areas developed were lands near the defense plants. During the nation's national defense period, 1940–1941, local developers worked at a fervent pace, leading the nation in the number new homes constructed.[4] Fred W. Marlow, a prominent home builder during the war, recalled, "We had a ready-made market. It wasn't a question of selling the houses, it was just a matter of

Large war plants, such as this Los Angeles aircraft plant, drew hundreds of thousands of hopeful workers to the Southland which in turn led to the city's severe wartime housing shortage. (Photograph courtesy of the University of Southern California's Regional History Center).

getting them up." Builders, such as Marlow and Fritz B. Burns, literally created new suburban communities. Among those built near the booming defense plants were Westside village (Mar Vista) near Douglas Aircraft in Santa Monica, Toluca Wood (North Hollywood) near Lockheed, and "Homes at Wholesale" (Westchester) near North American Aviation.

Home building, however, quickly slowed with the American entrance into the war. Builders found themselves stymied by wartime restrictions on building supplies and the loss of large numbers of their construction force to the war effort. Whereas private builders in Los Angeles had constructed an average of 45,000 private dwelling units each year in 1940 and 1941, construction dropped to less than 20,000 in 1942.[5] By June 1942, such previously growing communities as Glendale, Pasadena, Santa Monica, San Gabriel, and Alhambra saw their home construction rates drop to only one or two dwellings a month. The situation had become so bleak during November 1942 that building departments of three-fourths of the cities in Los Angeles County reported that no residential building permits of any kind had been issued.[6] As a result, the vacancy rate of all dwellings in Los Angeles County declined from 6 percent in April 1940 to a nominal 0.4 percent by July 1943.[7]

Especially hard hit by the region's housing shortages were areas surrounding defense plants and neighborhoods heavily populated by minorities. The housing shortage was particularly acute in the harbor district adjacent to the shipyards. The area, which became the work place of one-third of the war workers in Los Angeles, gained an estimated 92,000 persons between the attack on Pearl Harbor and the summer of 1943.[8] This 35 percent population transformed Long Beach into a major west coast city.

Although Long Beach had been a principal port for the United States Navy, it was nonetheless unprepared for the sudden onslaught of nearly 20,000 families in need of housing by the middle of 1943. Many of those unable to find adequate housing were forced to find shelter in cars or tents. Others, particularly those with large families, struggled to live in hotel rooms originally designed to house one or two people overnight. Life in these cramped quarters often forced young children to play outside in the streets or to become involved in activities which contributed to rising levels of juvenile delinquency. Unfortunately, the child care and school systems of Long Beach offered little in the way of relief for the children of war workers. Most child care centers were only open during the day, though the area's shipyards, using three shifts, worked around the clock. The school system, too, offered little hope since it lacked adequate facilities and faculty to handle the needs of the new arrivals. Ernest Debbs, State Assemblyman, spoke candidly of the community's situation: "Child welfare is bad, education is bad, school facilities are extremely bad."[9]

Central Los Angeles was also hard hit by the large-scale housing shortage. The inner city area, already notorious for congested and substandard housing, became home to the majority of blacks migrating to Los Angeles during the Second World War. Blacks were typically relegated to living within its confines out of financial necessity and because of racial covenants that prevented them from living in outlying white suburbs. With the monthly arrival of 10,000 to 12,000 black migrants in the summer of 1943, the already overwhelmed area became increasingly plagued with problems of crime and disease.[10]

Though belatedly, local and federal governments moved aggressively to solve Los Angeles' housing problem. Not only had the city become the nation's second largest defense producer in 1943, it had also become home to one out of every forty Americans.[11] The Los Angeles Regional Planning Commission worked together with the Federal Housing Authority to plan the needed housing for growing numbers of war workers and their families.

Remarkably, fifteen federally financed and owned housing developments were built by the summer of 1943. The most impressive of the fifteen was architect Richard J. Neutra's Channel Heights Project, built on a hillside overlooking the Pacific adjacent to the shipyards of San Pedro. The scenic 160-acre site had a density level of only 3.7 families per acre. The development included schools, nurseries, shops, a health center, a park area and a community hall.[12]

Despite the success of the Channel Heights Project, other federal housing projects in the Los Angeles area met with criticism on a variety of fronts. Transportation planners criticized the sites of several housing projects because they failed to locate near public transportation outlets.[13] Civil rights advocates condemned the housing policies of several of the projects because of their reluctance to house minorities.[14] Regardless of such criticism, Los Angeles during the war had the second largest wartime public housing program in the United States. The joint federal-city program built 33,000 units of public housing, which was three times the entire population of Los Angeles in 1880.

Ironically, while wartime Los Angeles continued to work on alleviating the region's housing shortage, it found itself contending with an overabundance of automobiles. With the highest number of automobiles

Despite nostalgic contentions to the contrary, trolley involved accidents were commonplace throughout wartime Los Angeles. (Photograph courtesy of the University of Southern California's Regional History Center).

per capita in the United States, Los Angeles grappled with numerous problems related to traffic congestion. Traffic gridlock was common during the war as thousands of cars competed with streetcars, buses and trucks on metropolitan streets.[15]

Adding to the traffic woes, was the presence of thousands of new arrivals who were unfamiliar with the city and its traffic regulations. Not surprisingly, the Los Angeles Police Department recorded a thirty-five percent increase in pedestrian injuries and deaths between 1939 and 1942.[16]

Much of the region's problems with traffic congestion was related to Los Angeles' decentralized base. The city's expansive size (450 square miles) for example, allowed workers who could not or did not want to live near defense plants the opportunity to commute from outlying areas. Commuting distances often proved to be substantial. Joseph H. Wadsworth of the California Shipbuilding Corporation estimated that 70 percent of the company's 40,000 workers commuted an average of 44 miles a day from their homes to work and back again.[17] Despite wartime restrictions on gasoline and tires, Los Angeles drivers remained entrenched in their use of automobiles. In April 1942, the California State Railroad Commission surveyed 225,000 Los Angeles industrial workers and found that an astonishing eighty-five percent travelled to work in private automobiles.[18]

In response, local city officials campaigned for workers to use carpools as both a means to aid the war effort and to help relieve the region's worsening traffic congestion. The officials, however, were disappointed to find their public relations campaign to have been a failure. Weary war workers continued to complain that distances between home and work were often too long for public transport ridership. Further, many complained that the street cars were noisy and uncomfortable. As evidence that the war did little to change public transportation ridership, passenger counts of cars travelling in Los Angeles in 1938 and 1945 showed only marginal increases in vehicle occupancy.[19]

In defense of private drivers, the automobile had been the principal means of transportation in Los Angeles since the early 1920s. The horizontal, rather than vertical, growth of the city encouraged automobile use. As car ridership gained popularity, local public transportation began to suffer significant fiscal losses. The Pacific Electric Railway which had already been in economic decline in the twenties, averaged losses of more than $2,000,000 a year from 1931 to 1940. The Los Angeles Railway (LARY) also suffered fiscal losses during the Depression. As a result, both companies began cutting back on needed capital improvements to their rail lines. By 1940, both had abandoned many of their railway franchises in the hopes of saving their businesses. The result was somewhat ironic. As the city continued to expand outward, miles of existing public transport were reduced by the fledgling companies.[20] As the region's population continued to dramatically increase, transportation planners were forced to contend with traffic bottlenecks that hindered the movement of war goods and workers. These bottlenecks were especially commonplace in city streets that led into such large aircraft plants as Douglas in Santa Monica and Lockheed in Burbank. The congestion became so bad at one point that city officials in Burbank closed all streets adjacent to the Lockheed plant and the city's airport.

The city's harbor area was also plagued with traffic woes. Delays frequently disrupted shipping schedules for transport of vitally needed war material overseas. Because of the port's difficult accessibility by land, military authorities continued to use San Francisco as the west coast's main military shipping depot despite Los Angeles' leadership in the manufacture and production of war goods.[21] Unfortunately, the onset of the war had halted work on several planned freeway projects that would have helped eased congestion near the port and many of the city's defense plants.[22]

Another difficulty faced by local government officials during the war years was the alteration of the property tax base. New arrivals were largely renters rather than homeowners, negatively affecting the city's property tax base. While the growing numbers of renters paid less in taxes they nonetheless needed the same level of municipal services as did local homeowners.[23] The tax base of the City of Los Angeles was further hurt by the continued movement of businesses and factories from the central city to surrounding suburban areas.

Other localities suffered as well. Extensive wartime acquisitions of municipal lands by the federal government further eroded the tax base of many of the region's cities.[24] Within Los Angeles County, the federal government acquired property then valued at nearly $700 million dollars.[25]

Having to meet increasing demands for municipal services despite substantial tax revenue loss angered Los Angeles Deputy Mayor Orville Caldwell. Appearing before the House Subcommittee on Congested Areas, Caldwell complained that:

> We have a burden here imposed upon us that we have been unable to cope with in that there has been a tremendous influx of people who have come to live within the city, for whom we have to maintain police protection, maintain the health department service; and yet we have no source of revenue from them whatsoever.[26]

The war's impact on municipal budgets forced several cities to demand assistance from the federal government. Because of its size and importance to the war effort, the City of Los Angeles received some federal help in providing police and fire protection in areas of the city inadequately served.[27] Nevertheless, these essential public services were still pushed to the breaking point throughout the region.

Loss of personnel to the military was especially difficult for the Los Angeles Police Department. Responsible in 1943 for the protection of an estimated population of 1,850,000 in an area of 450 square miles, the LAPD found itself short 530 sworn officers of its authorized strength of 2,547. Unable to replace 476 officers on military leave, due to civil service regulations, the Department was forced to undertake unusual measures to deal with an expanding crime rate, including the use of civilian volunteers (for traffic duty, office staffing, report taking), overtime duty for sworn officers, and reliance on military police to patrol areas frequented by service personnel.

Despite the emergency measures, crime rates reached new heights during the war years. In one year, between 1942 and 1943, felonious assaults and robberies increased more than 50 percent in Los Angeles. The Chief of Police blamed much of the rise on overcrowding. Particularly hard hit was the already congested black community of the central city. Many residents there found themselves dealing with growing crime rates while contending with problems of overt racism throughout the city.[28]

Long Beach, located in the congested harbor area, also experienced wartime increases in violent crime. According to its police chief, Walter H. Lentz, such incidents could be "attributed entirely to the war," although he admitted that the rate of crimes against property, such as burglary and theft, had shown actual decreases.[29] But like their counterparts in the LAPD, Long Beach police officials increasingly had to contend with problems not considered high priority, including public drunkenness, juvenile curfew violations, and vice-related offenses.

The problem of juvenile delinquency was most clearly linked to the war's impact. Between 1940 and 1943 the numbers of those arrested under 18 in Los Angeles doubled. The lack of proper parental supervision and overcrowded housing conditions contributed to the rise. The situation became so bad in parts of the city that parents of those repeatedly arrested were prosecuted for allowing their children on the streets again. Chief Horrall of the LAPD stated, however, that the results of these prosecutions had turned out to be "very unsatisfactory."[30] In fact, these kinds of crimes were considered likely to continue even if parents were prosecuted, because of the high incidence of parental absenteeism. The opportunity for both parents to work in high-paying defense jobs meant that all too often children went unsupervised.

The war also created unique challenges for police in the prosecution of vice-related offenses. Especially problematic was prostitution. Authorities were often stymied in their attempts to make arrests because many female prostitutes would only do business with men in uniform. Since police officers were prohibited from entrapping prostitutes by donning military uniforms, they turned to military officials for assistance. But much like the police themselves, military authorities complained they did not have the personnel to carry out the assignments.

The lack of properly trained and experienced personnel was a continual problem in the work places of wartime Los Angeles. However, the scarcity of trained emergency service personnel most concerned municipal authorities because it directly affected the safety and lives of those living in Los Angeles. The war's impact forced cities like Burbank and Compton to adjust their municipal budgets accordingly. Police officers' and firefighters' salaries were increased to make them more competitive with defense industry wages.[31] Adding to the woes of emergency authorities were War Production Board restrictions. Restrictive priority regulations hampered the ability to acquire badly needed equipment. Such shortages were common throughout Los Angeles.

The Los Angeles City Fire Department was one local emergency agency overwhelmed by the war's impact. While it lost nearly 500 personnel, between 1941 to 1943 the department experienced a 36 percent increase in emergency calls. The loss of experienced personnel not only hindered the department's fire fighting capabilities, it affected its ability

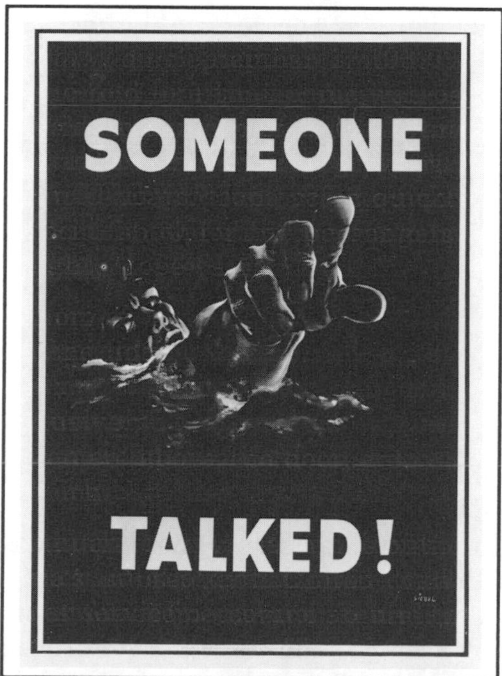

An often seen wartime poster warning citizens not to discuss the movement of troops. It was a particularly popular poster in the bars and war plants of Los Angeles. (Photograph courtesy of the National Archives)

to enforce fire safety laws. Fire Department officials, for example, discovered contractors for several government housing projects under construction had failed to comply with local fire safety codes. Upon inspection they found that many of the fire hydrants installed outside the buildings were not compatible with hoses carried on the city's fire engines.[32]

City and county health departments also encountered difficulties similar to those experienced by emergency services. Like their police and fire counterparts, Health Department administrators were forced to contend with shortages of qualified workers while meeting the demands of the city's increasing population. During the war, health administrators were responsible for battling sharp increases in sexually transmitted diseases, meeting the threats of possible citywide epidemics, and educating scores of newcomers in the values of proper sanitation.

Insufficient hospital space and outreach programs to meet public needs was a particularly difficult problem for public health officials. The shortage of adequate essential care facilities, for example, raised concerns that a serious epidemic in Los Angeles could affect the nation's war effort.

Such fears were not unfounded. Wartime Los Angeles received thousands of new residents and transients, a substantial percentage of whom had never been inoculated against communicable diseases. Further, overcrowding and lack of adequate sanitation in many parts of the region raised the threat of rodent- and insect-borne diseases such as bubonic plague, typhus fever, and malaria.[33]

Moreover, rapid wartime industrialization and population growth of Los Angeles created serious environmental problems. Most adversely affected were the adjacent Pacific Ocean and the air over Los Angeles. In terms of ocean pollution, Los Angeles' large population growth during the war years overtaxed regional sewer systems to the point that dumping of raw sewage in neighboring Santa Monica Bay became commonplace. The beaches of Southern California, the region's number one tourist attraction, were often closed during the war due to the presence of raw sewage grease along the shore. Elmer Belt, president of the California State Board of Health, complained of "massive, gross contamination" of the Los Angeles shoreline by the raw sewage, and he subsequently led efforts to quarantine beaches most seriously affected by sewage dumping. Still, the quarantines were not always effective and local Santa Monica Bay area doctors reported large increases in intestinal diseases in proportion to the numbers of ocean swimmers.[34]

Twelve–hour days and seven–day work weeks were not uncommon for war workers. Here a women war worker at Vultee Aircraft in Downey completes some tedious riveting work. (Photograph courtesy of the University of Southern California's Regional History Center)

Adding to public health woes was the dramatic wartime change in the region's air quality. Much of the change was due to the growth of new industries in the region. In 1940 and 1941 a total of 233 new industrial plants sprang up in Los Angeles. In the next two years industrial usage of the Los Angeles Department of Water and Power soared from 400,000,000 to over a billion kilowatt hours. Literally, while area production statistics brightened, the skies over Los Angeles darkened.[35]

The first noticeable traces of what later came to be known as smog came in the summer of 1940 when civic center workers complained of breathing difficulties and eye irritation. Investigation of the cause by public health officials of the recurring "abnormal atmospheric condition" proved inconclusive. By September 1942, the problem magnified, as outlying areas reported impaired visibility and increasing breathing difficulties.

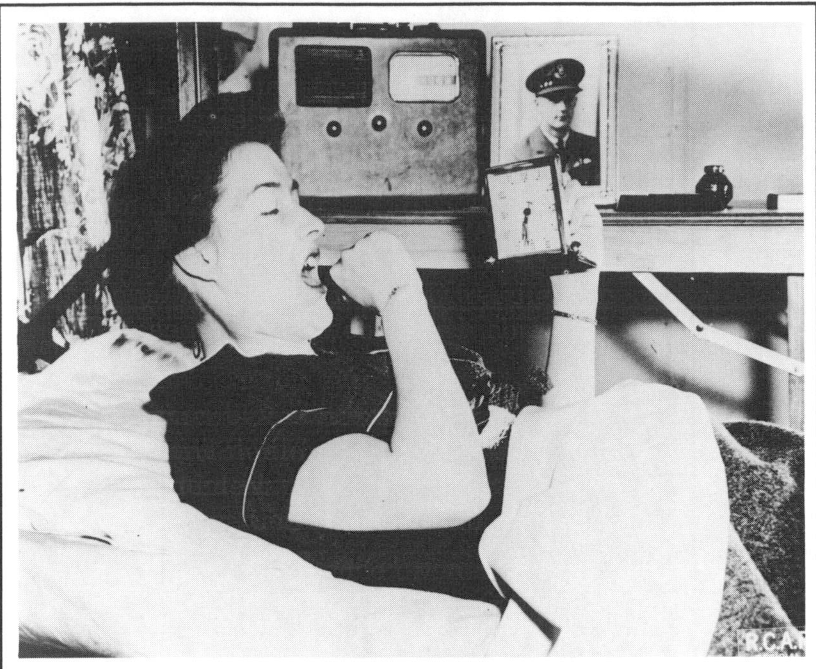

In a scene repeated thousands of times nightly in wartime Los Angeles, an exhausted war worker sets her alarm for the next day's shift. A nearby photo of a loved one in the military often served as special inspiration to keep working on the job for the war's conclusion. (Photograph courtesy of the National Archives)

Health workers began taking detailed air samples and not surprisingly identified a wide host of pollutants whose cause could be directly traced to industrialization and heavy automobile use. By the summer of 1943 the smog had become so thick in the downtown area that visibility was at times reduced to three city blocks.

The resultant smog hazard generated a public chorus of complaints to local politicians to do something about the deterioration of the city's air quality. On October 28, 1943 the County Board of Supervisors formed a five member County Smoke and Fume Commission to investigate ways to reduce the problems of smog. The Commission, meeting with business leaders and city and county officials, sought increased use of smoke abatement devices.[36] Unfortunately, use of these devices was not enough to end the problem. The industrialization of Los Angeles in conjunction with its topography and weather conditions created an inversion layer that trapped air pollutants thus condemning the city to a smoggy future.

In conclusion, the Second World War advanced the industrial growth of Los Angeles at the environmental expense of the city. This placed local political leaders in a difficult bind. If they fought against population growth, the chief contributor to the sewage problem, the region's economic progress would suffer. Similarly, curbing the sources of air pollution—industrialization and automobile use—would hurt war production.

Conflicts between local and federal authorities were not unusual in the battle between war production and the environment. In one case, Los Angeles city officials had to fight against the United States Navy for connecting a large sewer line into the city's treatment plant on Terminal Island. City officials argued that it was unfair that their already overburdened sewer system was expected to handle an additional 450,000 gallons a day from a naval base that wasn't even within the city limits of Los Angeles.[37] In addition, the Los Angeles City Council threatened legal action against the federal government's Rubber Reserve Corporation whose Aliso Street plant was considered the largest air polluter of the downtown area.[38]

Despite intergovernmental conflicts, the mutual interest in winning the war tended to override differences between local and federal officials. In attempting to solve the region's problems of congestion, pollution and a wide host of social ills, both government entities came to realize one another's great value to the war effort. Although the partnership did not fully solve the region's problems, Los Angeles nonetheless emerged from the war an industrial giant. The price Los Angeles would pay for its rapid wartime rise as a world leader in science and technology would overwhelm municipal infrastructures whose problems would often lead to social and environmental conflict over the region's limited resources.

Endnotes

1. Nash, *The American West Transformed,* p. 58.
2. 78th Cong., 2d sess., House, Subcommittee on Congested Areas, Subcommittee of Committee on Naval Affairs, *A Report of the Congested Areas Subcommittee of the Committee on Naval Affairs*, Report #144 (Washington, 1944), pp. 1193–1194.
3. Ibid., p. 1194.
4. 78th Congress, 2d sess., House, Subcommittee on Committee on Naval Affairs, *Hearings on Congested Areas* (8 parts, Washington, 1944), Part 8, p. 1973. Hereafter cited as *Congested Area Hearings.*
5. *Congested Area Hearings*, Part 8, p. 1973.
6. Security-First Bank, *Monthly Summary*, December 1942.
7. Ibid., and Arthur G. Coons and Arjay R. Miller, *An Economic and Industrial Survey of the Los Angeles and San Diego Areas* (Sacramento, California State Planning Board, 1941), p. 244.
8. *Congested Area Hearings*, Part 8, p. 1973.
9. Testimony of Ernest Debbs, State Registrar, Member of the State Legislature, *Congested Area Hearings,* Part 8, p. 1903.
10. Testimony of Orville R. Caldwell, Executive Deputy Mayor, City of Los Angeles, *Congested Area Hearings*, Part 8, p. 1761.
11. Ibid., p. 1761.
12. Martin Schiesl, "City Planning and the Federal Government in World War II: The Los Angeles Experience," *California History* 59:2 (April 1979), p. 132.
13. Testimony of Alfred H. Campion, Acting Chief Administrative Officer, County of Los Angeles, *Congested Area Hearings*, Part 8, p. 1781.
14. Quoted in Schiesl, "City Planning and the Federal Government in World War II," p. 132.
15. In 1940 there were 1,093,290 automobiles registered in Los Angeles County, the equivalent of one vehicle for each 2.54 persons. *Congested Area Hearings,* Part 8, p. 1781.
16. Testimony of C.B. Horrall, Chief of Police, City of Los Angeles, *Congested Area Hearings*, Part 8, p. 1770.

17. Testimony of Joseph H. Wadsworth, Director of Public Relations, California Shipbuilding Corporation, *Congested Area Hearings*, Part 8, p. 1907.

18. *Congested Area Hearings*, Part 8, p. 1781.

19. Scott L. Bottles, *Los Angeles and the Automobile: The Making of the Modern City* (Berkeley: University of California Press, 1977), p. 228.

20. The Los Angeles Railway did make a valiant effort in 1940 to improve its system by replacing its aging interurban street cars with buses. However, the subsequent wartime shortages of gasoline and tires eventually doomed the scheme.

21. Caldwell, *Congested Area Hearings*, Part 8, pp. 1760–1761.

22. *Investigation of Congested Areas*, Report #163, p. 1198.

23. In 1929, for example, 76 percent of the city's expenditures were financed by general property taxes. By 1943, property taxes only contributed 50 percent of the city's expenditures. *Congested Area Hearings*, Part 8, pp. 1760–1762.

24. *Investigation of Congested Areas*, Report #163, p. 1194.

25. Frank L. Kidner and Phillip Neff, *An Economic Survey of the Los Angeles Area* (Los Angeles: The Haynes Foundation, 1945), p. 98.

26. Caldwell, *Congested Area Hearings*, Part 8, p. 1762.

27. Nash, *The American West Transformed*, p. 66.

28. Horrall, *Congested Area Hearings*, Part 8, pp. 1770–1771.

29. Testimony of Walter H. Lentz, Chief of Police, Long Beach, CA., *Congested Area Hearings*, Part 8, pp. 1916–1917.

30. Horrall, *Congested Area Hearings*, Part 8, pp. 1770–1771.

31. *Investigation of Congested Areas*, Report #163, p. 1199.

32. Letter-report from John H. Aldelson, Chief Engineer, Department of Fire, City of Los Angeles, *Congested Area Hearings*, Part 8, pp. 1998–1999.

33. *Congested Area Hearings*, Part 8, pp. 1773–1780, 1816–1827.

34. Los Angeles *Times*, December 7, 1941; Elmer Belt, "A Sanitary Survey of Sewage Pollution of the Surf and Beaches of Santa Monica Bay," *Western City 19* (June 1943), pp. 17–22.

35. Marvin Brienes, "Smog Comes to Los Angeles," *Southern California Quarterly* 58:4 (1976), pp. 515–32.
36. Nash, *The American West Transformed*, p. 64.
37. *Congested Area Hearings*, Part 8, pp. 1760–1763.
38. Brienes, "Smog Comes to Los Angeles," p. 521.

Culture in Wartime Los Angeles

7

Prewar Los Angeles' reputation as a center of culture, measured in terms of art, drama, music, literary works and intellectual lifestyle, pale in comparison to the older cities of the East. During the war, however, the city made great strides in attaining cultural respectability. Film making, the region's predominant prewar cultural force, led the way, attracting to wartime Los Angeles some of the world's greatest literary, artistic, and intellectual talent. Their impact would forever enhance the city's cultural identity and help bring film making worldwide recognition as an important shaper of human culture and values.

During the war, Los Angeles remained the entertainment capital of the world. Radios around the globe would often be tuned to hear such popular Hollywood-produced programs as the "Jack Benny Show." Global listeners often delighted in hearing radio plots whose Hollywood and Beverly Hills scenarios conferred an almost magical feel to the environs of Los Angeles. Much of American military radio programming also called Los Angeles home. Originating many of its wartime programs from "Hollywood," the worldwide military broadcast network frequently entertained its vast G.I. audience with numerous Hollywood performers who volunteered their time and talents to entertain the troops.[1]

The most important financial component of the city's wartime entertainment industry, though, was movie making.[2] The industry's spectacular rise in a relatively short period of time was due to the overwhelming appeal of the "silver screen." As the industry grew and continued to evolve, public fascination with "Hollywood" remained fervent. In contrast to artistic expression commonly associated with high culture and privilege such as serious works of art, music, and poetry, movies were works of democratic mass culture. American movies made during the war served a variety of needs. They entertained, enlightened, boosted morale, and served to significantly shape the at-war consciousness of the American public.[3]

Even as war in Europe neared, public and media interest in the movie industry refused to wane. For example, in the late 1930s, some 400 news correspondents, including one representing the Vatican, covered the film industry in Hollywood. Only New York and Washington, D.C., had more reporters.[4] So powerful was the film industry's grip on the millions of weekly movie goers that its influence was strongly linked to fads in popular dress and hairstyles. Even foreigners succumbed to its influence. During the tumultuous "Battle of Britain," Londoners remained fixated on the sagas of their favorite Hollywood stars. Even during a blitz bombing, *The London Mirror*, wired its Hollywood correspondent for a two-hundred word piece on Ann Sheridan's contract dispute with Warner Brothers.[5]

Ironically, the movie industry's popularity created problems for Hollywood film makers. Chief among these were the Roosevelt administration's efforts to orchestrate support for its ideals through the popular medium. Attempts to propagandize movies were undertaken through the Office of War Information (OWI) and its subagency, the Bureau of Motion Pictures (BMP). Although President Franklin Roosevelt, in the days following the attack on Pearl Harbor, declared that he wanted "no censorship of the motion picture," he appointed his media aide Louis Mellett as head of the BMP. Mellett arrived in Hollywood in January 1942 and assured studio bosses that the Bureau of Motion Pictures would simply act as an advisory body to the film industry. To carry out its "advisory" task, Millett organized a staff of 140 employees with a $1.3 million dollar budget.[6]

One of the first wartime accomplishments of the BMP was issuance of a guidebook for studio film makers. Distributed in the summer of 1942, *The Government Information Manual for Motion Pictures* contained "suggestions" for movies that would aid the war effort. The guidelines, however, were framed in such a way as to promote wartime ideals of the Roosevelt administration. Despite the manual's ideological overtones, many Hollywood film makers followed its suggestions.[7]

Following the manual's publication, the BMP made a concerted effort to review movie scripts. Many film makers, in the spirit of patriotism and support for the war, turned their scripts over to the BMP for review. Although the movie industry was not legally obligated to carry out the BMP's requests, script writers duly incorporated the agency's suggestions. As a result, increasing numbers of film makers embraced ideological themes that emphasized democratic values and principles. They moved away from making movies that blatantly stereotyped the enemy or depictions of carefree civilian life. By the end of 1943, most films made in Hollywood met BMP specifications.[8]

Ironically, the BMP became a casualty of its own success. The agency's ability to influence the content of Hollywood movies raised concerns in the

From infantry, to planes, to ships, thousands of Hollywood studio workers participated in America's combat effort. Pictured is a SB2C Helldiver returning to the aircraft carrier *U.S.S. Yorktown* in July 1944. (Photograph courtesy of the National Archives)

film industry and in Congress. Film makers began objecting to the agency's growing demands and criticisms. Further, much of Hollywood was concerned with the agency's movement away from being a passive observer to being an active participant. In response to what they regarded as unfair interference, a growing number of film makers ignored the Bureau altogether. Congress, too, became concerned over the power of the federal agency. Fearing that the BMP had made the Hollywood movie industry into an effective propaganda tool for the Roosevelt administration, in May 1943 Congress cut the BMP's $1.3 million budget to a simple maintenance fund of $50,000.[9]

Congress' emasculation of the BMP program heightened film makers appreciation of the importance of their industry in shaping the national consciousness. In response, Hollywood shifted from making movies laden with political idealism to films that contained subtle messages in support of the war. Further, Hollywood film makers concentrated on providing moviegoers with much needed entertainment. In striking this balance,

Hollywood earned success at the box office and the gratitude of national leaders.

Another important wartime attribute of Hollywood was the patriotic contribution of those working within the industry. Although movie making was declared an "essential industry" by the Selective Service in February 1942, many working in the Hollywood studios stated openly that they did not want favored status.[10] By October 1942, nearly twelve percent of the industry's employees had entered the armed forces.[11] Among those volunteering with the cameramen, grips, writers, and electricians were some of Hollywood's biggest stars, including Clark Gable, Jimmy Stewart, Mickey Rooney, and Tyrone Power. The example set by major stars leaving large movie contracts to serve their country lifted the nation's morale and spurred military enlistment nationwide. While the military preferred to use movie stars to entertain troops, make training films, and selling war bonds, many screen personalities participated in the war as combatants.

The fact that movie stars were looked up to also proved beneficial in calming an understandably war-panicked public. Bob Hope, who was at sea aboard the *Queen Mary*, on September 1, 1939, was awakened late that night by his wife who told him that panic was beginning to grip the passengers. That evening's announcement that France and Britain had just declared war on Germany had created growing fears that the ship would be sunk by German U-boats. Hope acted quickly to ease passenger fears by putting on a special show for the passengers. As the ship sailed through the darkened night, Hope sang,

> Thanks for the memory,
> Some folks slept on the floor,
> Some in the corridor;
> But I was more exclusive,
> My room had 'Gentlemen' above the door,
> Ah! Thank you so much.[12]

His appearance did much to take the minds of the passengers off the problems at hand. Hope's subsequent United Services Organizations (U.S.O.) wartime shows for service personnel around the world earned him the esteem and appreciation of millions of troops.

Other stars in the industry also went beyond the call of duty to aid the war effort. Many travelled thousands of miles to entertain troops or toured around the United States to raise money for war bonds. Female movie stars proved particularly adept at raising the much needed revenue. Hedy Lamarr offered to kiss any man who would buy $25,000 worth of war bonds. In one day she sold $17 million. Dorothy Lamour was estimated to have sold more than $350 million worth of bonds during the war years. And sadly, Carole Lombard, wife of Clark Gable, lost her life in a plane crash on the way home from a bond-raising drive.[13]

Hollywood also did its part to show its appreciation for those serving in uniform. The movie industry worked hard to accommodate the thousands of troops that wanted to see Hollywood before they departed for combat in the Pacific. Studio tours were held, special shows were given, and even swimming pool parties were thrown at movie stars' homes.[14] But the most popular attraction among troops in Hollywood was its nightlife.

To accommodate the many servicemen without money or female companionship, the Hollywood Canteen was developed. The building of a safe Hollywood night club for G.I.s came under the direction of actress Bette Davis. With the help of volunteer studio workmen, Davis converted

Clark Gable and his famous actress wife Carole Lombard at the popular Los Angeles club Florentine Gardens. Just a few days after this photo was taken, Mrs. Gable would lose her life in a tragic plane crash while returning to Los Angeles from a war bond-raising drive. A despondent Gable soon enlisted himself in the Army as a private. (Photograph courtesy of the University of Southern California's Regional History Center).

a barn off Sunset Boulevard into what became the social center of Hollywood. Miss Davis obtained financial support for the Canteen through donations from the movie industry. Her biggest success, however, was getting movie stars to help in its operation. Top names provided entertainment and company for the hundreds of G.I.s who showed up nightly.

It was not unusual to see the movie stars washing dishes, cleaning tables or just making small talk with Canteen visitors. When the Canteen swung, as it usually did, many once lonely G.I.s found themselves dancing with famous Hollywood starlets. For many soldiers, it would be one of the few fond memories of the war.[15]

While the Canteen provided an entertaining refuge for visiting soldiers, it also proved to be a publicity bonanza for Hollywood. Movie executives and stars alike found themselves depicted positively in newspapers throughout the world. The club itself became the source of a 1944

Like millions of other Americans, Mayor Bowron took time on June 6, 1944 to pray for the safety of Allied troops as they began the D-Day invasion of Normandy, France. (Photograph courtesy of the University of Southern California's Regional History Center).

Warner Brother's movie, aptly titled HOLLYWOOD CANTEEN. Self-serving or not, the Canteen gave stars and troops a much needed place to go.

Hollywood used the war to its best advantage. Studio bosses sought to protect their product by emphasizing to their employees the importance of favorable publicity and positive public relations. Within sixty days of the American declaration of war, the movie industry had given 1200 16-mm prints of current features and shorts in 90-minute programs to the War Department for free showings to American combat soldiers.[16] The effort did not go unpublicized. Not only did the donation earn Hollywood favorable press, it helped the industry to maintain its market place with the troops overseas. On any given day during the war it was estimated that 1,150,000 troops attended more than 3,000 film showings.[17]

Hollywood portrayed itself as a tireless resource in the war effort. This was not done entirely for altruistic reasons. Even after the Bureau of Motion Pictures (BMP) was discarded by Congress in May 1943, the industry had to contend with government regulators in order to export its films. The government succeeded in convincing the industry to follow regulations that would portray the United States and its ambitions in a positive light. Instead of fighting the government over issues of regulation and censorship, the movie industry conceded to government demands in order to insure uninterrupted production. By doing so studios were able to increase their foreign markets while earning favorable publicity.

Despite loss of studio personnel, rationing and government regulation, the movie industry flourished during the war period. Much of its success was possible because high wartime employment gave the American people more discretionary money to spend, while at the same time rationing and curtailment of production of civilian goods limited the products they could purchase. With the closing of many nightclubs and racetracks, money spent by Americans on entertainment often flowed into studio coffers instead. Studio profits were further increased through the enforcement of government restrictions that limited the amount of money spent on making movies. By sharing movable sets, recycling costumes, and limiting the amount of film used in production, studios saved costs and thereby increased profits. In the short space of five years, industrywide pretax profits rose dramatically from $52 million in 1940 to $261 million in 1944.[18]

The war also brought to the movie industry some of its greatest talent. According to cultural historian Peter Gay, "The exiles Hitler made were the greatest collection of transplanted intellect, talent, and scholarship the world has ever seen."[19] Hollywood attracted part of the exiled talent because of the employment opportunities it offered for writers, musicians and artists. Further, the film community itself offered financial support for the exiles through its European Relief Fund.

Many in the film community were themselves European emigrés. Their successful adaptation to Los Angeles and the movie industry proved encouraging to hundreds of gifted exiles. Among those who had arrived before the war were Billy Wilder, Ernst Lubitsch, Ernst Toch, and Paul Kohner. Lubitsch, who had lived in Los Angeles since 1930, had become one of Hollywood's top directors. His stature in the community was such that, "a telephone call from Ernst Lubitsch had the same effect as a summons from a king."[20] Lubitsch convinced dozens of Hollywood personalities to donate one percent of their salaries to the European Relief Fund. Ernst Toch, an esteemed composer, attracted similarly talented musicians to the industry. He diligently worked at getting signed affidavits pledging support for refugees in case the newcomers experienced financial hardships. Paul Kohner, another German emigré, used his influence as a top Hollywood agent to meet with several movie studio presidents. Kohner explained to the studio moguls the fate awaiting Germany's best writers at the hands of the Nazis. In one day, Kohner obtained twenty one-year screen writing contracts for the refugee writers.[21]

The efforts of the emigré community and the film industry attracted a wide variety of European notables. Although the number of European war refugees in Southern California totaled no more than ten thousand, they nonetheless proceeded to give Los Angeles added cultural identity.[22] Their adjustment to Los Angeles, however, was not always smooth. Used to diligently working on projects of high culture, the refugee artists found Los Angeles to be mass culture oriented. Many refugees arriving in the Southland denounced the region's lack of sophistication. The great composer Arnold Schoenberg once described an advertisement he had come across while living in Los Angeles as an insight into the culture of the city. He wrote to a close friend:

> There's a picture of a man who has run over a child, which is lying dead in front of his car. He clutches his head in despair, but not to say anything like: "My God, what have I done?" For there is a caption saying: "Sorry, now it is too late to worry—take out your policy at the XX Insurance Company in time." And these are the people I'm supposed to teach composition to![23]

Despite problems of adjustment, both trivial and profound, many refugees remained committed to producing works of high culture. Although Los Angeles lacked the sophistication of the great cities of Europe from which they had fled, many of these talented emigrés found the area conducive to the work. In fact, several were pleasantly surprised to find their works receiving a broad and warm reception through the mass culture media of movies and radio.[24]

One of the areas most impacted by the European emigrés' arrival was the field of music. Attracted by excellent salaries and job opportunities, some of Europe's greatest musicians relocated to Los Angeles. From studio orchestras to film composition, emigré musicians and composers brought forth classical tradition while introducing new contemporary music to the masses. Not only did the emigrés reach audiences through film, many performed in the Los Angeles Philharmonic as well. The Philharmonic was often led by the famous German conductor, Bruno Walter, and the orchestra helped Los Angeles to obtain international cultural recognition.[25]

The city's major universities profited from the musicians as well. Joining the music faculty of the University of Southern California were the noted composers Ernst Toch, Ingolf Dahl, Ernest Gold and Ernst Kanitz. The University of California at Los Angeles obtained the services of the renowned composer Arnold Schoenberg. Many of the emigrés' students went on to become famous musicians themselves.[26]

Many of the musicians succeeded remarkably well in their adaptation to Los Angeles. The ability of music to transcend language barriers allowed the emigrés to perform to their highest standards. Since many participated in the composing and arranging of film scores, they found their works reaching a worldwide audience. According to emigré composer Erich Wolfgang Korngold's wife, her husband received great satisfaction in receiving widespread recognition from his musical film scores. She recalled, "Thousands of letters arrived from all over the United States, later even from Europe and South America.... Korngold fan clubs were founded; Erich received gifts from all parts of the United States at Christmas and on his birthday."[27]

The success of the emigré musicians could be seen in the hundreds of Hollywood film scores they composed and arranged. Several, including Korngold and Ernest Gold, won academy awards for their exceptional work. By contrast, many emigré writers arriving in Los Angeles to work in the studios found themselves hindered by language and cultural barriers. Forced to write in the closed confines of studio writing departments, the exiled writers quickly learned that their work was not done as an individual pursuit. Movie scripts were such that the story line passed through the hands of many writers before its completion. Many exiled writers found their creativity and vitality sapped by the studio experience. Thus, even though the pay was attractive, most emigré writers quit after their one-year contracts ran out.[28]

Due to the war, the emigré writers also had to contend with the loss of their reading audiences. Since most of the writers continued to write in their native languages, they also had difficulty obtaining publishers for their works. Famous emigré authors who fell on hard times in Los Angeles included Alfred Doeblin, Hendrich Mann (brother of Thomas), and Bertolt Brecht. The feeling of exile permeated much of their wartime writing.[29]

Other European emigrés sought to combat their feelings of isolation by banding together. In fact, the growth of a strong literary group in Los Angeles attracted other emigré writers to the area. The most successful of the transplanted authors was Thomas Mann. Already prominent in the literary community for such novels as *The Magic Mountain* and *Buddenbrooks*, Mann often acted as a host to other emigré writers and artists. Among the many visitors to Mann's home was the great Russian composer and fellow Los Angeles resident, Igor Stravinsky. Further, on many nights at Mann's home there would be gathered some of the world's greatest literary talent. Erich Maria Remarque, author of *All Quiet on the Western Front*, was a frequent visitor as was Franz Werfel, author of *The Song of Bernadette*.[30]

Another Pacific Palisades resident was the famous novelist and short story writer Lion Feuchtwanger, who as a war emigré himself, delighted in entertaining fellow emigré writers. His wife, affectionately called Frau Marta, served apfel strudel with whipped cream to the guests in their home as they happily recreated for the emigrés a home away from home.

As in film and music, the gathering of literary talent also brought Los Angeles international recognition. Since the 1930s the movie industry had been luring some of America's greatest writers to Los Angeles. Among them were F. Scott Fitzgerald, William Faulkner, Ernest Hemingway, Robert Sherwood, and S.J. Perelman. Hollywood also lured from England Aldous Huxley, Somerset Maugham, and Evelyn Waugh.[31] Thus, with a distinguished literary group already in place, along with the movie industry's ability to provide employment, it was understandable so many emigré writers decided to live in Los Angeles.

Despite complaints that the studio writing was too confining or that the area's temperate weather sapped their vitality, many emigré writers continued to produce important works while in Los Angeles. Both Thomas Mann and the frustrated Bertolt Brecht did some of their best work there during the war. While many emigré writers were unable to make the adaptation to screen writing others fared quite well. Among those who did were Fredrich Kohner (brother of Paul), Walter Reich, and Robert Thoeren.[32]

Several emigré writers living in Los Angeles even began to write for American audiences. One of the most successful was Fredrich Kohner. His humorous experience in raising a daughter in the beach-dominated environment of Southern California led to his writing the immensely popular novel, *Gidget* in 1957.[33] Thus, despite problems with adaptation to Los Angeles' way of life, many emigré writers gave the city's growing literary community an international flavor and added prestige.

European emigrés also made substantial contributions to the Los Angeles art scene. Many emigrés in positions as art collectors, gallery owners, museum curators and academics helped Los Angeles to develop an appreciation of European classical art.[34] The emigrés also encouraged Los Angeles to embrace modern art. The influence of these connoisseurs contributed to Los Angeles' maturation into one of the world's leading art centers.[35]

Local science and medicine also benefited from the emigrés' work. At the California Institute of Technology the work of German emigré Max Delbrueck made the institution the world's leader in genetics research.[36] Hans Reichenbach at UCLA and Heinrich Gompertz at USC introduced Los Angeles to the highly specialized study of science as a philosophy.[37] Even psychoanalysis gained a strong foothold in Los Angeles under the direction of Ernst Simmel. Simmel, originally from Berlin, was both a dynamic teacher and brilliant scholar. Many of the techniques of psychoanalysis he helped develop were subsequently used to aid people affected by war neuroses. His work also helped individuals battling drug and alcohol addictions.[38]

Although the war emigrés to Los Angeles totaled no more than 10,000, their influence on the intellectual development of Los Angeles was significant. They were instrumental in "ridding" the city of its cultural provincialism. Their impact helped Los Angeles to become internationally recognized as a center of literary and musical talent. Further, their influence in developing an appreciation of art and furthering the pursuit of academic scholarship enabled Los Angeles to garner increasing recognition as a "cultured city." Further, the influence of the city's movie industry would continue to bring Los Angeles national and international attention. Not only did the industry help maintain the nation's morale during the war, but its movies became recognized as an important shaper of American thought and values.

Endnotes

1. Curtis Mitchell, *Cavalcade of Broadcasting* (Chicago: Follett Publishing Company, 1970), p. 142.
2. Otto Friedrich, *City of Nets: A Portrait of Hollywood in the 1940s* (New York: Harper and Row, 1986), p. 14.
3. Dwight MacDonald, "A Theory of Mass Culture," in Bernard Rosenberg and David Manning White (eds.), *Mass Culture: The Popular Arts in America* (Glencoe, IL: The Free Press, 1957), pp. 59–73; Edward Shils, "Mass Society and its Culture," in Bernard Rosenberg and David Manning White (eds.), *Mass Culture Revisited* (New York: Van Nostrand Reinhold Company, 1971), pp. 64–65.
4. Clayton R. Koppes and Gregory D. Black, *Hollywood Goes to War: How Politics, Profits, and Propaganda Shaped World War 2 Movies* (New York: Macmillan, 1987), pp. 12–13.
5. Ibid., p. 13.
6. Ibid., p. 70, John Morton Blum, *V Was for Victory: Politics and American Culture During World War II* (New York: Harcourt Brace Jovanovich, 1977), pp. 24–25.
7. Friedrich, *City of Nets*, p. 211.
8. Allan M. Winkler, *The Politics of Propaganda: The Office of War Information, 1942–1945* (New Haven: Yale University Press, 1978), pp. 57–60. Friedrich, *City of Nets*, p. 211.
9. Ibid.
10. Ken Jowett, *Film: The Democratic Art* (Boston: Little, Brown and Company, 1976), p. 311.
11. Richard Lingeman, *Don't You Know There's a War On ? The American Home Front, 1941–1945* (New York: G.P. Putnam's Sons), p. 170.
12. Friedrich, *City of Nets*, pp. 25–26.
13. Ibid., pp. 106–107.
14. Los Angeles *Times*, Special Mid-Winter Edition, January 3, 1944.
15. Friedrich, *City of Nets*, p. 108.
16. Report by the War Activities Committee, "The Industry at War," *The Hollywood Reporter*, Twelfth Anniversary Issue, October 1942.

17. *Movie Lot to Beachhead* (Editors of *Look*), (New York: Doubleday, Doran and Co., 1945), p. 104.

18. Tino Balio, *United Artists: The Company Built by the Stars* (Madison: The University of Wisconsin Press, 1976), p. 171.

19. Peter Gay, "Weimar Culture: The Outsider as Insider," in Donald Fleming and Bernard Bailyn (eds.), *The Intellectual Migration* (Cambridge: Harvard University Press, 1969), pp. 11–12.

20. As quoted in Jarrell C. Jackman, "Exiles in Paradise: A Cultural History of German Emigrés in Southern California, 1933–1950" (Ph.D. dissertation, University of California, Santa Barbara, 1977), p. 90. Jarrell C. Jackman's dissertation is summarized in, "Exiles in Paradise: German Emigrés in Southern California, 1933–1950," *Southern California Quarterly*, vol. 61 (Summer, 1979), p. 183–203.

21. Jackman, "Exiles in Paradise: A Cultural History," pp. 90–91.

22. Nash, *The American West Transformed*, p. 195.

23. Arnold Schoenberg, *Letters*, selected and edited by Erwin Stein (New York: St. Martin's Press, 1965), p. 242

24. Nash, *The American West Transformed*, p. 195.

25. Ibid., pp. 193–194.

26. Ibid., p. 195.

27. As quoted in Jackman, "Exiles in Paradise: A Cultural History," p. 196.

28. Ibid., pp. 92–97.

29. "German Emigrés in Southern California," in Jarrell C. Jackman and Carla M. Borden (eds.), *The Muses Flee Hitler: Cultural Transfer and Adaptation 1930–1945* (Washington: Smithsonian Institution Press, 1983), p. 96.

30. Nash, *The American West Transformed*, p. 189.

31. Jackman, "Exiles in Paradise: A Cultural History," p. 113.

32. Ibid., pp. 108–109.

33. Jackman, "German Emigrés in Southern California," in *The Muses Flee Hitler*, p. 102.

34. Carla Higins, “Art Collecting in the Los Angeles Area, 1910–1960” (Ph.D. dissertation, University of California at Los Angeles, 1963), pp. 238–239.

35. Nash, *The American West Transformed*, p. 193.

36. Ibid., p. 166.

37. Ibid., p. 196.

38. Ibid., p. 170–171.

Epilogue

8

WASHINGTON, Aug. 14. (U.P.) – **Japan surrendered unconditionally tonight, bringing peace to the world after the bloodiest conflict mankind has known.**[1]

The announcement of Japan's surrender at 4:00 p.m. (P.S.T.) sent thousands of joyous Angelenos out into the city's downtown streets. As swarms of office workers and shoppers hugged, kissed, and danced together, some celebrants were observed falling to their knees in a brief prayer of thankfulness.

The city's joy remained unabated throughout the following months as hundreds of thousands of troops were returned to American soil at the

Raising the flag atop Mt. Suribachi, February 23, 1945. Three of the flag raisers would soon lose their lives in the savage battle to take the Japanese held island of Iwo Jima. (Photograph courtesy of the National Archives)

The British liner Queen Mary, filled to capacity with returning American troops, arrives in New York Harbor, June 20, 1945. The Queen Mary would later become a popular Los Angeles tourist attraction. (Photograph courtesy of the National Archives)

city's port entrance.[2] As organizations, such as the Red Cross, struggled to handle the 500,000 new troop arrivals in the four months following the war's conclusion, civic leaders, through interviews and newspaper accounts, discovered that many of the returning G.I.s planned to remain permanently in the Southland. In addition, due to the city's unprecedented prosperity, thousands of soon-to-be-residents continued to arrive from other states. Post-war newspaper headlines such as "California, Here They Come!," which were accompanied by photos of long lines of cars at state border stations, became commonplace. In response to the continued population explosion, local municipal authorities in the immediate postwar months worked feverishly to expand the city's already overtaxed infrastructure. Among the first postwar civic improvements was an expansion of the city's municipal airport and the adjacent beach side construction of a massive sewage treatment plant (Hyperion).

Despite housing shortages and crowded streets and stores, Angelenos seemed to revel in a postwar euphoria. Part of their shared happiness centered on the city itself and all that it had to offer. One new postwar arrival wrote in the Los Angeles *Times*, "I have just come from Europe. When I walk in Los Angeles and see the wonderful stores and the food, which for the moment is more interesting than clothes... I want the American people to know that this is heaven on earth." Echoing the sentiments of many returned war veterans the writer continued, "Every day when I wake up and see the sun shining I have happiness in my heart and sometimes I am afraid I shall wake up and find it is all a dream. But no, dear editor, as I look out my window on 60th St. and see the beautiful view I realize that I am here all right. I want to make my home here and never leave it again."[3]

Los Angeles emerged from the Second World War as the leading city of the newly industrialized west. Although the cessation of hostilities in 1945 prompted fears that Los Angeles would be plagued by war plant closures and large unemployment, the city's ties to technological innovation assured it of a bright future. Just as the city quickly adapted itself to

Joyous "vets" excitedly await their return to American soil. A two-day delay at Long Beach caused some of the anxious troops to threaten to storm off their ships as they had done when they invaded Japanese held islands. (Photograph courtesy of the National Archives)

wartime production, it rapidly and successfully adjusted to a postwar economy.

Los Angeles, however, between 1939 and 1945 had been dramatically changed by the war. Its emergence as the nation's second leading defense producer brought with it problems of overcrowding, traffic congestion, and environmental pollution. On the bright side, a wartime partnership with the federal government had enabled Los Angeles to reduce its historical dependence on the East for finished goods and industrial financing. The success of this partnership was translated into the employment of thousands of workers and the production of defense goods that helped the Allies win the war.

The Second World War changed nearly every facet of life in Los Angeles. Some of the most dramatic changes occurred in the expansion of local industry. Although some 175,000 wage earners were dropped from local manufacturer's payrolls between August 1944 and September 1945, substantial wartime employment gains were retained in nearly every local industry.[4] The aircraft industry, for example, at its lowest postwar employment level was still nearly 400 percent above its 1939 prewar level.[5] The shipbuilding industry, which suffered an 81 percent decline in employment between its wartime peak and October 1945, nevertheless exceeded its 1939 level by over 500 percent. Other industries experiencing substantial growth during the war years (petroleum, steel, and electric), survived postwar downturns in employment only to quickly recover with dramatic gains over their 1939 prewar levels.[6] The growth of local industry was so substantial that even as production reached its lowest postwar levels in December 1945, local manufacturing employment exceeded that of 1939 by nearly 80 percent.[7]

Among the chief factors influencing the wartime industrial growth of Los Angeles were federal government investment capital, a large work force, and the region's abundant natural resources. The federal government's interest in developing industry in Los Angeles stemmed from the city's location and its manufacturing potential. Located adjacent to the tense Pacific theatre, Los Angeles was separated from the more industrialized East by approximately three thousand miles. Despite its isolation, Los Angeles by 1937 ranked fifth among American cities in the value of its manufactured products and third in the number of manufacturing establishments. Between 1939 and 1945 the city's industries and businesses received over $11 billion dollars in war contracts.[8]

Los Angeles proved worthy of Federal investment dollars. The area's several hundred small concerns, which characterized the manufacturing base of Los Angeles in 1939, quickly converted to wartime production needs. They proved instrumental in supplementing the needs of the area's most important wartime industries: aircraft production and shipbuilding.

The infusion of federal defense dollars during the war years rescued Los Angeles' ailing shipbuilding industry. During its wartime peak, the industry expanded dramatically to employ ninety thousand workers, or nearly 100 times the workers employed in 1939.[9] Los Angeles shipyards during the war handled more than one and one-half billion dollars in shipbuilding contracts.[10]

The chief recipient of federal defense dollars, however, was the aircraft industry. In the short space of five years, employment rolls in the industry climbed from 13,330 in January 1939 to more than 228,000 by the summer of 1944.[11] As testimony to the aircraft industry's value to the war effort, Los Angeles County received nearly half of the five billion federal dollars spent in California between June 1940 and July 1942.[12] The vast majority of this money was used to pay for aircraft orders and to finance further growth and development of the industry.[13]

Federal defense dollars also were used to finance industries that produced locally needed unfinished items, especially those requiring steel and aluminum. Perhaps most notable was the federally financed Kaiser steel plant in Fontana. The Fontana mill, second largest in the west, helped Los Angeles to break the domination of eastern-based industries whose high cost for raw and basic materials hindered the city's industrial development. As a result of these investments, Los Angeles emerged from the war confident that it could produce locally many of the items needed to carry on its expansive industrial program.

Los Angeles' confidence in its postwar future was further spurred by the wartime gains made in harnessing the abundant natural resources of the area. Substantial progress was made in oil recovery, chemical and electrical production. In addition, gains made in technological developments added to the city's growing industrial strength. The most important natural resource, though, was the people of Los Angeles. Despite wartime stresses and strains, many Angelenos worked well beyond the 48-hour average work week. Still others worked the mandatory 48-hour work week and then used their free time as civilian defense volunteers. Despite these heroic efforts, there never seemed to be enough workers to meet wartime industrial needs. The chronic shortages were eased only by the constant influx of first-time workers.

Previously neglected groups, notably women, blacks, and Hispanics, made their way aggressively into the ranks of well-paying occupations for the first time, representing social changes that bordered on revolutionary. For the first time in the history of Los Angeles, these groups worked in large numbers in positions that had been dominated by white males. At the height of wartime production, the labor force in the aircraft industry was 42 percent women. Blacks and Hispanics also made dramatic employment gains. Blacks, who had experienced the most blatant discrimination before the war, comprised three to seven percent of the wartime work forces at various aircraft plants. Although each of these groups experienced sharp downturns in employment near the end of the war due to the return of white male workers, fiscal cutbacks, and other cultural and social factors, maintenance of second-class status for women and minorities thereafter was unacceptable to both groups.[14]

The federal government played an important role in helping women and minorities obtain employment in the wartime industries of Los Angeles. Through its chief agency for minority groups, the Fair Employment Practices Commission (F.E.P.C.), the government exerted pressure on employers to end discriminatory hiring practices. Although the agency was considered weak and ineffective, its hearings on working conditions and labor practices encouraged minority groups to continue their fight for equal employment. The intervention of the federal government on their behalf kept growing numbers of minorities committed to the ideals of democracy.

An important aspect in the fight for equal employment and working conditions was the continued development of organized minority groups. Groups such as the Negro Victory Committee achieved important gains for their causes. By maintaining a mainstream patriotic strategy, these groups were able to press their demands for job opportunities. Among their successful approaches were large war bond rallies, where organization leaders not only raised money for the war but also pleaded for war industry jobs for minorities. The irony of large worker shortages and the continued refusal by industries to hire minorities was not lost on the press or the public. Pressure such as this helped open up jobs in the continually worker-short Los Angeles Railway Corporation.

Minority community organizations also played a vital role in pointing out the problems of their communities exacerbated by the war. Minority community leaders, such as Charlotta Bass, editor and publisher of the black newspaper, The California *Eagle*, made known the needs and problems in the black community by serving on public boards and organizing peaceful protests.[15] Although government help remained limited, inroads were made in the segregated and discriminatory features of Los Angeles society. One of the most important new starts was the work begun to end housing covenant restrictions. Strong efforts to repeal this policy were begun in the minority communities during the war years when the racially segregated communities were overrun with immigrants.[16]

The federal government through its senate and congressional investigations also shed light on the growing problems of minorities in wartime Los Angeles. Chief among these problems were overcrowding, crime and the lack of adequate health care facilities in minority communities. The wide availability of war work in Los Angeles' attractive setting brought thousands of immigrants into the area. Although Los Angeles was accustomed to population booms, the wartime population growth occurred without the commensurate increases in housing and public services. As a result, crime and disease rates showed significant rises during the war.[17]

The vast migration of aspiring war workers and their families dramatically altered the population characteristics of the Los Angeles area. The United States Bureau of the Census in January 1946 conducted a special census of Los Angeles City. It found that the total population had grown by 20 percent since 1940. The female population grew by 22.9 percent while the number of males increased by 17.1 percent.[18]

The substantial increase in the number of women can best be explained by the large numbers who came to Los Angeles in search of war work, and because thousands of men from Los Angeles were still in the armed services at the time of the survey. The most dramatic changes, however, occurred in the minority communities. The black community grew by an astounding 108.7 percent. In contrast, mostly due to the removal of the Japanese-Americans, other racial groups not classified under white or black (except for Hispanics who were classified by census takers as white), declined by nearly half.[19]

As a result of the strong population growth of the city of Los Angeles and an estimated wartime population growth of 31 percent for Los Angeles County, the region appeared destined for a bright future.[20] Adding to the bright picture were the easing of restrictions on building materials. With plenty of open space remaining outside the central city, Los Angeles expected to handle its burgeoning population growth by building new residences. During the first nine months of 1945, a total of 21,916 building permits were issued by the city, a number more than double that of either Detroit or New York City.[21]

Another positive indicator of Los Angeles' postwar economic strength was the large-scale conversion of war production plants into peacetime factories. During the last four months of 1945, $55 million dollars were spent on converting or building new factories in Los Angeles. This was two-thirds more than the expenditure in the first nine months of 1945, and it exceeded expenditures for any full year in the history of the area except for the war years, 1941–1943.[22] Many of those buying and converting war plants were companies from outside the region. During the war, 31 eastern and midwestern manufacturers bought property in Los Angeles County. Following the war's conclusion, such companies as Sylvania Electric, General Motors and Quaker Oats all opened up large branch factories in Los Angeles. Approximately one-eighth of all the new businesses started in the United States in 1946 were begun in Southern California, thus adding to the region's economic promise.[23]

Hollywood legend Jimmy Stewart attempted to quietly return to Los Angeles. The humble Stewart earned the Distinguished Flying Cross, six battle stars, and the Croix de Guerre. (Photograph courtesy of the University of Southern California's Regional History Center).

Despite the termination of large war contracts following the war's conclusion in August 1945, Los Angeles retained its close ties with the federal government. Among the key developments emanating from the war experience was the establishment of a large aerospace industry in Southern California with an important economic relationship with the military. At the war's conclusion, military authorities chose Los Angeles as the site for the government's first "think tank," the RAND Corporation. Standing for "Research and Development," the Rand Corporation brought military authorities and scientists together to discuss military contingencies and defense strategies.[24]

Los Angeles also emerged from the war a leading fashion center. Between 1940 and 1945 employment in the city's garment industry grew by approximately 20 percent. Ironically, the greatest boom during the war in the garment industry came not from its tremendous production of parachutes, life preservers, and military outfits, but in the production of clothing that reflected the outdoor and informal living style characteristic of Los Angeles. Among the best individual customers were visiting military personnel, many of whom were taken with the region's temperate climate and natural beauty.[25]

The wartime success of Los Angeles' garment industry reflects the city's popularity beyond its borders. During the war years Los Angeles was seen as a Mecca for those seeking work, warmth and a lifestyle conducive to informal living. Blacks from the Deep South, in particular, came to Los Angeles in record numbers in search of both jobs and the chance to escape the rigid racial stratification of the South. Young women also found Los Angeles conducive to beginning independent lives. War work in Los Angeles paid well and the city offered a good nightlife as well. The city's entertainment industry lured some of the world's greatest talent to Los Angeles, offering them high-paying work and a place of refuge from the destruction of Europe. Thus, the emigres' presence helped Los Angeles ascend to the ranks of one of the world's cultured cities later in the postwar era.

Upon the war's conclusion, Los Angeles remained a popular destination for those in search of better lives and economic opportunity. Even with the city's well-publicized problems of smog filled air, congested streets, inadequate housing, racial tension and a broken sewer system to name but a few of the wartime afflictions, newcomers continued to pour in. Much of the city's attraction remained the industrial base that had been developed by the war. No longer dependent on the investment monies and raw materials from the regions east of the Rockies, Los Angeles, in partnership with the federal government, developed a self-sustaining

A Coast Guardsman silently remembers a comrade who wouldn't be coming home. Over 290,000 American troops died in combat during the Second World War. (Photograph courtesy of the National Archives)

economy that was oriented toward future regional growth and technological innovation.

Betting on that future were record numbers of migrants that continued to arrive in the months following the war. So large were their numbers that by 1943, Los Angeles had become home to one in forty Americans.[26] And unlike most war boom areas, Los Angeles' new inhabitants decided to remain in the city. Indeed, many invited friends and relatives to join them. This new population of footloose people sought government housing and jobs and looked for the urban advantages of good schools, pleasant neighborhoods, and a California life-style of automobiles and easy access to work, shops, and recreation. The Second World War thus gave them a taste of paradise. As the Los Angeles *Times* explained in late December 1945,

> The story of the west's great industrial future has spread over the nation and like the story of the discovery of gold, it is luring hopeful men whose dreams are spun of golden opportunity.[27]

That opportunity awaited them in Los Angeles.

Endnotes

1. Los Angeles *Times*, August 15, 1945.

2. As late as December 17, 1945, the Port of Los Angeles was handling an average of 20,000 service personnel arrivals daily. So overwhelmed were local authorities that "two-day waits" to get off the ships was not uncommon. At one point, an understandably impatient group of war hardened veterans threatened to storm ashore as they had done against the Japanese held islands in the Pacific.

3. Los Angeles *Times*, December 17, 1945.

4. Frank L. Kidner and Phillip Neff, *Los Angeles: The Economic Outlook* (Los Angeles: The Haynes Foundation, 1946), p. 5. Particularly hard hit by aircraft industry lay-offs were thousands of women defense workers. A postwar survey conducted by the Los Angeles *Times* found that the number of women in the city's five largest aircraft plants had dropped from thirty-seven percent on August 5, 1945 to twenty-seven percent by December 16, 1945. While it is true that some of these women left voluntarily, other women found themselves forcibly removed from company payrolls by lay-off notices and social mores that demanded that returning male war veterans be given any available jobs in the high-paying industry.

5. James Richard Wilburn, "Social and Economic Aspects of the Aircraft Industry in Metropolitan Los Angeles During World War II," (Ph.D. dissertation, University of California, Los Angeles, 1971), p. 247.

6. Security-First National Bank of Los Angeles, *Monthly Summary of Business Conditions in Southern California*, December 1946.

7. Ibid., January 1946.

8. Los Angeles *Times*, Special Mid-Winter edition, January 2, 1946.

9. Los Angeles' shipyards employed approximately 1,000 workers in 1939.

10. Arthur G. Coons and Arjay R. Miller. *An Economic and Industrial Survey of Los Angeles and San Diego Areas* (Sacramento: California State Planning Board, 1941), p. 198.

11. Wilburn, "The Aircraft Industry in Metropolitan Los Angeles During World War II," p. 247.

12. Los Angeles County received 47.1 percent of the five billion federal dollars spent in California between June 1940 and July 1942.
13. Security-First National Bank, *Monthly Summary*, August 1942.
14. Wilburn, "The Aircraft Industry in Metropolitan Los Angeles During World War II," pp. 236–237.
15. Charlotta Bass, *Forty Years: Memoirs from the Pages of a Newspaper* (Los Angeles, 1960).
16. The United States Supreme Court in 1948 ruled in *Shelley v. Kraemer* and *Hurd v. Hodge* that the enforcement of restrictive covenants against selling residential properties to minorities was in violation of the 14th Amendment and the Civil Rights Act of 1866. A Los Angeles case, *Barrows v. Jackson* (1953), closed an important loophole by ruling out damage suits against the seller of a property covered by restrictive covenant. For description and background on the Los Angeles case, see Loren Miller, "Scotching Restrictive Covenants," in John and LaRee Caughey, eds., *Los Angeles: Biography of a City* (Berkeley: University of California Press, 1976), pp. 388–391.
17. 78th Congress, 2d sess., House Subcommittee on Committee on Naval Affairs, *Hearings on Congested Areas* (8 parts, Washington, 1944), Part 8, pp. 1770–1780, 1816–1827.
18. Special U.S. Census figures on population characteristics of Los Angeles City on January 28, 1946 are broken down in Security-First National Bank, *Monthly Summary*, September 1946.
19. Ibid.
20. Ibid.
21. In comparison, Detroit was ranked second nationally with 9,965 permits followed by New York City with 9,707. Los Angeles *Times*, Special Mid-Winter Edition, January 2, 1946.
22. Security-First National Bank, *Monthly Summary*, February, 1946.
23. "The Undiscovered City." *Fortune 39* (June, 1949), p. 160.
24. Fred Kaplan, "Scientists at War: The Birth of the RAND Corporation," *American Heritage* 34:4 (1983), pp. 49–64.
25. The garment industry in Los Angeles in 1944 employed 35,000 workers and had sales of $265 million dollars. Although New York still dominated the industry, strong inroads were made during the

war years. By 1944, the industry was selling 85 percent of its product east of the Rockies. Carey McWilliams, *California the Great Exception*, (New York: A.A. Wyn, 1949), pp. 218–220; Takuji Tamaru, "An Analysis of the Factors Which Have Influenced the Location of the Apparel Industry in Los Angeles," (Masters thesis, University of Southern California, 1951), pp. 65–96; "Los Angeles' Little Cutters," *Fortune 31* (May 1945), pp. 134–9.

26. *Hearings on Congested Areas*, Part 8, p. 1761.

27. Los Angeles *Times*, December 18, 1945.

❑ Selected Bibliography ❑

Books

Abbott, Carl. *The New Urban America: Growth and Politics in Sunbelt Cities*. Chapel Hill: University of North Carolina Press, 1982.

Ainsworth, Ed. *Out of the Noose! Way Pointed for American Cities to Save Themselves From Traffic Stagnation*. Los Angeles: Automobile Club of Southern California, 1938.

Anderson, Fred. *Northrop: An Aeronautical History*. Los Angeles: Northrop Corporation, 1976.

Anderson, E. Frederick. *The Development of Leadership and Organization Building in the Black Community of Los Angeles from 1900 Through World War II*. Saratoga: Twenty-Century One Publishing, 1982.

Anderson, Karen. *Wartime Women: Sex Roles, Family Relations, and the Status of Women During World War II*. Westport: Greenwood Press, 1981.

Archibald, Katherine. *Wartime Shipyard: A Study in Social Disunity*. Berkeley: University of California Press, 1947.

Balio, Tino. *United Artists: The Company Built by the Stars*. Madison: The University of Wisconsin Press, 1976.

Bain, Joe S. *War and Postwar Developments in the Southern California Petroleum Industry*. Berkeley: University of California Press, 1945.

Baruch, Dorothy. *Glass House of Prejudice*. New York: W. Morrow & Company, 1946.

Bass, Charlotta. *Forty Years: Memoirs from the Pages of a Newspaper*. Los Angeles: California Eagle, 1960.

Bemis, George W. *Intergovernmental Coordination of Public Works Programs in the Los Angeles Metropolitan Area*. The Haynes Foundation, *Pamphlet Series No. 10*, Los Angeles, 1945.

Berge, Wendell. *Economic Freedom for the West*. Lincoln: University of Nebraska Press, 1946.

Berkin, Carol R. and Lovett, Clara M. (eds.). *Women, War, and Revolution*. New York: Holmes and Meier, 1980.

Biddle, Wayne. *Barons of the Sky: The Story of the American Aerospace Industry*. New York: Simon and Schuster, 1991.

Bigger, Richard and Kitchen, James D. *How the Cities Grew: A Century of Municipal Independence and Expansionism in Metropolitan Los Angeles*. Los Angeles, 1952. *Metropolitan Los Angeles, A Study in Integration*, Vol. II, The Haynes Foundation, *Monograph Series No. 19*.

Blake, Aldrich. *You Wear the Big Shoe: An Inquiry into the Politics and Government of the American City, with a Case Study of the Los Angeles Metropolitan Area*. Los Angeles: By the Author, 1945.

Blum, John M. *'V' Was for Victory: Politics and American Culture During World War II*. New York: Harcourt, Brace & Jovanich, 1976.

Blumenson, Martin. *Patton: The Man Behind the Legend, 1885–1945* (New York: William Morrow and Company, 1985), pp. 160–161.

Bogardus, Emory S. *Southern California, a Center of Culture*. Los Angeles: University of Southern California, 1940.

Bottles, Scott L. *Los Angeles and the Automobile: The Making of the Modern City*. Berkeley: University of California Press, 1987.

Brinkley, David. *Washington Goes to War*. New York: Alfred A. Knoph, 1988.

Brownlow, Kevin and Suber, Howard. *The War, the West, and the Wilderness*. New York: Knopf, 1979.

Buchanan, A. Russell. *Black Americans in World War II*. Santa Barbara, CA: American Bibliographical Center–Clio Press 1977.

Bunker, John Gorley. Liberty Ships: *The Ugly Ducklings of World War II*. Annapolis: Naval Institute Press, 1972.

Campbell, D'Ann. *Women at War with America: Private Lives in a Patriotic Era*. Cambridge: Harvard University Press, 1984.

Caughey, John and LaRaee. *Los Angeles: Biography of a City*. Berkeley: University of California Press, 1976.

Central Business District Association. *Los Angeles Transit Study, Los Angeles Metropolitan Area*. Los Angeles, 1944.

Chafe, William. *The American Woman: Her Changing Social, Economic, and Political Roles, 1920–1970*. New York: Oxford University Press, 1972.

Collins, Keith E. *Black Los Angeles: The Maturing of the Ghetto, 1940–1950*. Saratoga: Twenty Century One Publishing, 1980.

Commonwealth Club of California. *The Population of California*. San Francisco: California Research Service, 1946.

Congress of Industrial Organizations. Industrial Union Councils, California. *The CIO Reports on the War*. Los Angeles: CIO, 1943.

Coons, Arthur G. and Miller, Arjay R. *An Economic and Industrial Survey of the Los Angeles and San Diego Areas*. Sacramento: California State Planning Board, 1941.

Coordinator of Inter–American Affairs. *Spanish-Speaking Americans in the War: The Southwest*. Washington: Coordinator of Inter–American Affairs and Office of War Information, 1943.

Craig, Richard B. *The Bracero Program*. Austin: University of Texas Press, 1971.

Cunningham, Frank. *Skymaster: The Story of Donald Douglas*. Philadelphia: Dorrance and Company, 1943.

Cunningham, William G. *The Aircraft Industry: A Study in Industrial Location*. Los Angeles: Lorrin L. Morrison, 1951.

Daniels, Roger. *The Decision to Relocate the Japanese*. Malabar, FL.: R.E. Krieger Publishing Company, 1975.

Dockson, R. R. *Growth Patterns: The Dynamic Los Angeles Area*. Los Angeles: The Haynes Foundation, 1958.

Downtown Business Men's Association of Los Angeles. *Retailers for Victory*. Los Angeles: Privately printed, 1943.

Draper, Harold. *Jim–Crow in Los Angeles*. Los Angeles: Workers Party, 1946.

Eberle, George J. "The Business District" in *Los Angeles: Preface to a Master Plan*. Ed. by George W. Robbins and L. Deming Tilton. Los Angeles, 1941. Pp. 127–44.

Finkle, Lee. *Forum for Protest: The Black Press During World War II*. Cranbury, NJ: Fairleigh Dickinson University Press, 1975.

Finney, Guy Woodward. *Angel City in Turmoil*. Los Angeles: American Press, 1945.

Fisher, Lloyd E. *The Problem of Violence: Observations on Race Conflict in Los Angeles*. Chicago: American Council on Race Relations, 1946.

Fleming, Donald and Bailyn, Bernard (eds.). *The Intellectual Migration*. Cambridge: University of Harvard Press, 1969.

Ford, John. *Thirty Explosive Years in Los Angeles County*. San Marino: Huntington Library, 1961.

Friedrich, Otto. *City of Nets: A Portrait of Hollywood in the 1940s*. New York: Harper and Row, 1987.

Funigiello, Philip J. *The Challenge to Urban Liberalism: Federal–City Relations During World War II*. Knoxville: University of Tennessee Press, 1978.

Fussell, Paul. *Wartime: Understanding and Behavior in the Second World War*. New York: Oxford University Press, 1989.

Gabler, Neal. *An Empire of Their Own: How the Jews Invented Hollywood*. New York: Crown Publishers, Inc. 1988.

Gallup, George. *The Gallup Poll: Public Opinion, 1935–1971*. New York: Random House, 1972.

Garfinkel, Herman. *When Negroes March: The March on Washington Movement in the Organizational Politics for F.E.P.C.* Glencoe, IL: Free Press, 1959.

Girder, Audie and Loftis, Anne. *The Great Betrayal: The Evacuation of the Japanese-Americans During World War II*. New York: Macmillan Company, 1969.

Gluck, Sherna Berger. *Rosie the Riveter Revisited: Women, the War, and Social Change*. Boston: Twayne Publishers, 1987.

Gordon, Margaret S. *Employment Expansion and Population Growth: The California Experience, 1900–1950*. Berkeley: University of California Press, 1954.

Gorter, Wytze and Hildebrand, George H. *The Pacific Coast Maritime Shipping Industry, 1930–48*. Berkeley: University of California Press, 1952–54. 2 vols.

Gottlieb, Robert. *Thinking Big: The Story of the Los Angeles Times, Its Publishers and Their Influence on Southern California*. New York: G. P. Putnam's Sons, 1977.

Gray, Robert D. *Systematic Wage Administration in the Southern California Aircraft Industry*. New York: Industrial Relations Counselors Incorporated, 1943.

Gregory, Ross. *America 1941: A Nation at the Crossroads*. New York: Macmillan Publishers, 1989.

Grodzins, Morton. *Americans Betrayed: Politics and the Japanese Evacuation*. Chicago: University of Chicago Press, 1949.

Gunston, Bill. *Aircraft of World War II*. New York: Crescent Books, 1980.

Hanson, Earl. *Los Angeles County Population and Housing Data: Statistical Data from the 1940 Census*. Los Angeles: The Haynes Foundation, 1944.

Hanson, Earl and Beckett, Paul. *Los Angeles: Its People and Its Homes*. Los Angeles, 1944.

Harris, Mark J.; Mitchell, Franklin D.; and Schecter, Steven. *The Homefront: America During World War II*. New York: G.P. Putnam's Sons, 1984.

Henstell, Bruce. *Sunshine and Wealth: Los Angeles in the Twenties and Thirties*. San Francisco: Chronicle Books, 1984.

Hill, Herbert. *Black Labor and the American Legal System: Race, Work and the Law*. University of Wisconsin Press, 1985.

Holtzman, Abraham. *Los Angeles County Chief Administrative Officer: Ten Years' Experience*. Bureau of Governmental Research, University of California, Los Angeles, *Studies in Local Government No. 10*. Los Angeles, 1948.

Hundley, Norris. *The Great Thirst: Californians and Water, 1770's–1990's*. Berkeley: University of California Press, 1992.

Jackman, Jarrell C. and Borden, Carla M. (eds.). *The Muses Flee Hitler: Cultural Transfer and Adaptation 1930–1945*. Washington: Smithsonian Institution Press, 1983.

Janeway, Eliot. *The Struggle for Survival: A Chronicle of Economic Mobilization in World War II*. New Haven: Yale University Press, 1951.

Jones, Helen L. and Wilcox, Robert F. under the direction of Edwin A. Cottrell. *Metropolitan Los Angeles: Its Governments*. Los Angeles: The Haynes Foundation, 1949.

Jowett, Ken. *Film: The Democratic Art*. Boston: Little, Brown and Company, 1976.

Kasun, Jacqueline Rorabeck. *Some Social Aspects of Business Cycles in the Los Angeles Area, 1920–1950*. Los Angeles: Haynes Foundation, 1954.

Kessleman, Louis C. *The Social Politics of F.E.P.C.: A Study in Reform Pressure Movements*. Chapel Hill: University of North Carolina Press, 1948.

Ketchum, Richard M. *The Borrowed Years, 1938–1941: America on the Way to War*. New York: Random House, 1989.

Ketcham, Ronald M. *Intergovernmental Cooperation in the Los Angeles Area*. Bureau of Governmental Research, University of California, Los Angeles, *Studies in Local Government No. 4*. Los Angeles, 1940.

Kidner, Frank Le Roy and Neff, Philip. *Los Angeles, the Economic Outlook*. Los Angeles: The Haynes Foundation, 1945.

Koppes, Clayton R. and Black, Gregory D. *Hollywood Goes to War: How Politics, Profits, and Propaganda Shaped World War II Movies*. New York: Macmillan, 1987.

Lebo, Harlan. *Casablanca: Behind the Scenes*. New York: Simon and Schuster, 1992.

Lewin, Molly (ed.). *The City of Los Angeles, the First 100 Years, 1850–1950*. Los Angeles: The Haynes Foundation, 1950.

Lewin, Molly and Shevsky, Eshref. *Your Neighborhood, A Social Profile of Los Angeles*. Los Angeles: The Haynes Foundation, 1949.

Lichtenstein, Nelson. *Labors War at Home: The CIO in World War II*. Cambridge, England: Cambridge University Press, 1982.

Lilley, Tom, et al. *Problems of Accelerating Aircraft Production During World War II*. Cambridge: Harvard University Press, 1946.

Lingeman, Richard R. *Don't You Know There's a War On? The American Home Front, 1941–1945*. New York: G. P. Putnam's Sons, 1970.

Look Magazine, (eds.). *Movie Lot to Beachhead, the Motion Picture Goes to War and Prepares for the Future*. Garden City, NJ, 1945.

Lotchin, Roger W. *Fortress California, 1910–1961: From Warfare to Welfare*. New York: Oxford University Press, 1992.

Mazon, Mauricio. *The Psychology of Symbolic Annihilation: The Zoot–Suit Riots*. Austin: University of Texas Press, 1984.

McEntire, Davis. *The Labor Force in California: A Study of Characteristics and Trends in Labor Force Employment and Occupations in California, 1900–1950*. Berkeley: University of California Press, 1952.

McWilliams, Carey. *Brothers Under the Skin*. Boston: Little, Brown and Company, 1943.

McWilliams, Carey. *California: The Great Exception*. New York: A. A. Wyn, 1949.

McWilliams, Carey. *Ill Fares the Land: Migrants and Migratory Labor in the United States*. Boston: Little, Brown and Company, 1942.

McWilliams, Carey. *Prejudice. Japanese–Americans: Symbol of Racial Intolerance*. Boston: Little, Brown and Company, 1944.

McWilliams, Carey. *Southern California Country: An Island on the Land*. New York: Duell, Sloan & Pearce, 1946.

Mitchell, Curtis. *Cavalcade of Broadcasting*. Chicago: Follett Publishing Company, 1970.

Modell, John. *The Economics and Politics of Racial Accommodation: The Japanese of Los Angeles, 1900–1942*. Urbana: University of Illinois Press, 1977.

Modley, Rudolf (ed.). *Aircraft Facts and Figures, 1945*. New York: McGraw and Hill Book Company, 1945.

Mullins, William H. *The Depression and the Urban West Coast, 1929–1933*. Bloomington: Indiana University Press, 1991.

Myrdal, Gunnar. *An American Dilemma: The Negro Problem and Modern Democracy* New York: Harper and Brothers, 1944.

Nash, Gerald D. *The American West in the Twentieth Century*. Albuquerque: University of New Mexico Press, 1977.

Nash, Gerald D. *The American West Transformed: The Impact of the Second World War*. Bloomington: Indiana University Press, 1985.

Nash, Gerald, D. (ed.). *The Urban West*. Kansas: Sunflower University Press, 1979.

Nash, Gerald D. *U.S. Oil Policy, 1890–1964: Business and Government in Twentieth Century America*. Pittsburgh: Pittsburgh University Press, 1968.

Nash, Gerald D. *World War 2 and the West: Reshaping the Economy*. Lincoln: University of Nebraska Press, 1989.

Neff, Philip and Weifenbach, Annetts. *Business Cycles in Los Angeles*. Los Angeles: The Haynes Foundation, 1949.

Neff, Philip; Baum, Lisette C. and Heilman, Grace E. *Favored Industries in Los Angeles*. Los Angeles: The Haynes Foundation, 1948.

Nelson, Donald M. *Arsenal of Democracy: The Story of American War Production*. New York: Harcourt, Brace and Company, 1946.

Newlin, Dika. *Schoenberg Remembered: Diaries and Recollections, 1938–1976*. New York: Pendragon Press, 1980.

Northrup, Herbert R. *The Negro in the Aerospace Industry*. Philadelphia: University of Pennsylvania Press, 1968.

Northrup, Herbert R. *Organized Labor and the Negro*. New York: Harper and Brothers, 1944.

Nunis, Doyce B. (ed.). *Los Angeles and Its Environs in the Twentieth Century: A Bibliograpy of a Metropolis*. Compiled under the auspices of the Los Angeles Metropolitan History Project. Los Angeles: Ward Richie Press, 1973.

Ogburn, William Fielding (ed.). *American Society in Wartime*. Chicago: University of Chicago Press, 1943.

Perrett, Geoffrey. *Days of Sadness, Years of Triumph: The American People, 1939–1945*. New York: Coward, McCann and Geoghegan, 1973.

Perry, Louis B. and Perry, Richard S. *A History of the Los Angeles Labor Movement, 1911–1941*. Los Angeles: University of California, 1963.

Polenberg, Richard (ed.). *America at War: The Home Front, 1941–1945*. Englewood Cliffs, NJ: Prentice–Hall, 1968.

Polenberg, Richard. *War and Society: The United States, 1941–1945*. Critical Periods of History. Philadelphia: J. B. Lippincott, 1972.

Powdermaker, Hortense. *Hollywood: The Dream Factory*. Boston: Brown, Little and Company, 1950.

Queenan, Charles F. *The Port of Los Angeles: From Wilderness to World Port*. Los Angeles: Los Angeles Harbor Department, 1982.

Rae, John B. *Climb to Greatness: The American Aircraft Industry, 1920–1960*. Cambridge: MIT Press, 1968.

Rand, Christopher. *Los Angeles: The Ultimate City*. New York: Oxford University Press, 1967.

Robbins, George W. and Tilton, L. Deming (eds.). *Los Angeles: Preface to a Master Plan*. Los Angeles: The Pacific Southwest Academy, 1941.

Rolle, Andrew F. *Los Angeles: From Pueblo to City of the Future*. San Francisco: Boyd and Fraser Press, 1981.

Romo, Richard. *East Los Angeles: History of a Barrio*. Austin: University of Texas Press, 1983.

Rosenberg, Bernard and White, David Manning (eds.). *Mass Culture: The Popular Arts in America*. Glencoe IL.: The Free Press, 1957.

Rosenberg, Bernard and White, David Manning (eds.). *Mass Culture Revisited*. New York: Van Nostrand Reinhold Company, 1971

Ruchames, Louis. *Race, Jobs, and Politics: The F.E.P.C.* New York: Columbia University Press, 1953.

Rupp, Leila J. *Mobilizing Women for War: German and American Propaganda, 1939–1945*. Princeton: University Press, 1979.

Satterfield, Archie. *The Homefront: An Oral History of the War Years in America, 1941–1945*. Chicago: Playboy Press, 1981.

Schoenberg, Arnold. *Letters*. Selected and edited by Stein, Erwin. New York: St. Martin's Press, 1965.

Scott, Mellier G. *Metropolitan Los Angeles: One Community*. Los Angeles: The Haynes Foundation, 1949.

Shevky, Eshref. *The Social Areas of Los Angeles, Analysis and Typology*. Los Angeles: The Haynes Foundation, 1949.

Shevky, Eshref and Lewin, Molly. *Your Neighborhood: A Social Profile of Los Angeles*. The Haynes Foundation, *Pamphlet Series No. 14*. Los Angeles, 1950.

Smith, Calvin C. *War and Wartime Changes: The Transformation of Arkansas, 1940–1945*. Fayetteville: The University of Arkansas, 1986.

Smith, Jack. *Jack Smith's L.A.* New York: McGraw–Hill, 1980.

Starr, Kevin. *Material Dreams: Southern California the 1920's*. New York: Oxford University Press, 1990.

Stewart, Irvin. *Organizing Scientific Research for War*. Boston: Little, Brown and Company, 1948.

Stimson, Grace H. *Rise of the Labor Movement in Los Angeles*. Berkeley: University of California Press, 1955.

Taylor, Frank J., and Wright, Lawton. *Democracy's Air Arsenal*. New York: Duell, Sloan, and Pearce, 1947.

TenBroek, Jacobus; Barnhart, E. N. and Matson, F. W. *Prejudice, War, and the Constitution and Consequences of the Evacuation of Japanese Americans in World War II*. Berkeley: University of California Press, 1958.

Thomas, Dorothy S. and Nishimoto, Richard S. *The Spoilage*. Berkeley: University of California Press, 1946.

Thomas, Lately. *Storming Heaven: The Lives and Turmoils of Minnie Kennedy and Aimee Semple McPherson*. New York: Morrow Publishing Company, 1970.

Viertel, Salka. *The Kindness of Strangers*. New York: Random House, 1969.

Warner, Jack. *My First Hundred Years in Hollywood*. New York: Random House, 1965.

Webber, Bert. *Silent Siege: Japanese Attacks Against North America in World War II*. Fairfield, WA.: Ye Galleon Press, 1984.

Webber, Bert. *Retaliation: Japanese Attack and Allied Countermeasures on the Pacific Coast in World War II*. Corvallis: Oregon State University Press, 1975.

White, Gerald T. *Billions for Defense: Government Financing by the Defense Plant Corporation During World War II*. University, Ala.: University of Alabama, 1982.

Wilcox, Robert F. and Jones, Helen L. *Metropolitan Los Angeles*. Los Angeles: The Haynes Foundation, 1949.

Winkler, Allan M. *The Politics of Propaganda: The Office of War Information, 1942–1945*. New Haven: Yale University Press, 1978.

Woll, Allen L. *The Hollywood Musical Goes to War*. Chicago: Nelson–Hall, 1983.

Wollenberg, Charles. *Ethnic Conflict in California History*. Los Angeles: Tinnon–Brown, Inc. 1970.

Wynn, Neil A. *The Afro–American and the Second World War*. New York: Holmes and Meier, 1976.

Zierer, Clifford M. (ed.). *California and the Southwest*. New York: John Wiley and Sons, 1956.

Zuckmayer, Carl. *A Part of Myself*. New York: Morrow, 1970.

Manuscripts

Bowron, Fletcher. Papers. Henry L. Hunington Library, San Marino, California.

Ford, Anson L. Papers. Henry L. Hunington Library, San Marino, California.

Los Angeles Urban League, 1940–1945. Special Collections, University of California, Los Angeles. Collection 203.

McWilliams, Carey. Carey McWilliams Collection, Number 2, Vertical Files, University of California, Los Angeles.

Articles

Arroyo, Luis Leobardo. "Chicano Participation in Organized Labor: The CIO in Los Angeles, 1938–1950." *Aztlan* 6:2 (Summer 1975): 276–303.

Belt, Elmer. "Sanitary Survey of Sewage Pollution of Santa Monica Bay." *Western City, 19* (June 1943): 17–22.

Black, Gregory D. and Koppes, Clayton R. "OWI Goes to the Movies: The Bureau of Intelligence Criticism of Hollywood, 1942–43." *Prologue, 6* (Spring 1974): 49–55.

Blum, John Morton. "United Against: American Culture and Society during World War II." *Harmon Memorial Lectures in Military History*, 25 (1983): 1–12.

"Bowron's Boom Town." *Time, 52* (October 11, 1948): 27–8.

Beigel, Harvey M. "The Battle Fleet's Home Port." *Proceedings* (History Supplement 1985): 54–63.

Brienes, Marvin. "Smog Comes to Los Angeles," *Southern California Quarterly* 58:4 (1976): 515–532.

Butterfield, Roger. "Los Angeles Is The Damndest Place, the City That Started With Nothing But Sunshine Now Expects to Become the Biggest in World." *Life, 15* (November 22, 1943): 102–4+.

"City of the Angels: Aviation's Boom Town." *Fortune, 23* (March 1941): 90–5+.

"City Planning: Battle of the Approaches." *Fortune, 28* (November 1943): 164–68, 222–23.

"Civilian Defense in Los Angeles." *Western City, 18* (September 1942): 20–43+.

Dalfiume, Richard M. "The Forgotten Years of the Negro Revolution." *Journal of American History, 55* (June 1968): 90–106.

DeGraaf, Lawrence B. "Recognition, Racism, and Reflections on the Writing of Western Black History." *Pacific Historical Review, 44* (May 1975): 22–51.

Elliott, Arlene. "The Rise of Aeronautics in California, 1849–1940." *Southern California Quarterly, 52* (1970): 1–32.

"Enlisting Citizen Cooperation for Sewage Treatment and Other Coastline Improvements." *American City, 60* (February 1945): 78.

"Fashion Warfare: Los Angeles Boosts Fund to Sell City as Style Capital of the World." *Business Week* (March 25, 1944): 48.

Garcia, Mario T. "Americans All: The Mexican Generation and the Politics of Wartime Los Angeles." *Social Science Quarterly* 65:2 (June 1984): 278–289.

Gill, Corringon. "Five Congested Productions Areas Designated on West Coast." *Western City, 20* (February 1944): 25–6.

Gluck, Sherna Berger. "Interlude or Change." *International Journal of Oral History* 3:2 (1981): 92–113.

Gressley, Gene M. "Colonialism and the American West." *Pacific Northwest Quarterly, 54* (January 1963): 1–8.

Hamerow, Theodore S. "Women, Propaganda, and Total War." *Reviews in American History* 7:1 (1979): 122–7.

Harris, Mark Jonathon; Mitchell, Franklin D., Schecter, Steven J. "Rosie the Riveter Remembers." *American Heritage* 35:2 (1984): 94–103.

Harris, William H. "Federal Intervention in Union Discrimination: F.E.P.C. and West Coast Shipyards during World War II." *Labor History* 22:3 (1981): 325–347.

Hildebrand, George and Mace, Arthur Jr. "The Employment Multiplier in an Expanding Industrial Market: Los Angeles County, 1940–47." *Review of Economics and Statistics, 32* (August 1950): 241–9.

Himes, Chester B. "Zoot Riots Are Race Riots." *Crises* 50:7 (July 1943).

Jackman, Jarrell C. *Southern California Quarterly* 61:2 (Summer 1979): 183–203.

Kaplan, Fred. "Scientists at War: The Birth of the Rand Corporation." *American Heritage* 34:4 (1983): 49–64.

Kessler–Harris, Alice. "'Rosie the Riveter': Who Was She?" *Labor History* 24:2 (1983): 249–53.

Koppes, Clayton R. and Black, Gregory D. "What to Show the World: The Office of War Information and Hollywood, 1942–1945." *Journal of American History, 64* (June 1977): 87–105.

Lively, Bruce R. "Naval and Marine Corps Reserve Center, Los Angeles." *Southern California Quarterly*, LXIX (Fall 1987): 241–254.

"Los Angeles at 160." *Newsweek, 18* (September 15, 1941): 16–7.

"Los Angeles: Forgotten Sun." *Newsweek, 28* (December 23, 1946): 27.

"Los Angeles Gets Ready." *Time, 38* (December 15, 1941): 76+.

"Los Angeles' Little Cutters," *Fortune, 31* (May 1945): 134–9+.

"The Los Angeles Spirit." *Time, 45* (January 1, 1945): 58–9.

Mezerick, A. G. "West Coast Versus East." *Atlantic Monthly, 173* (May 1944): 48–52.

Miller, Marc. "Working Women and World War II." *New England Quarterly* 53:1 (March 1980): 52–61.

Motley, Willard F. "Small Town Los Angeles." *Commonweal, 30* (June 30, 1939): 251–2.

Okihiro, Gary Y. and Sly, Julie. "The Press, Japanese Americans, and the Concentration Camps." *Phylon* 44:1 (1983): 66–83.

Perry, George S. "The Cities of America: Los Angeles." *Saturday Evening Post, 218* (December 15, 1945): 14–5+.

"Quarantine of Beach from Pollution Reduces Use to Minimum." *Western City, 20* (February 1944): 19.

Saxton, Alexander. "World War II: Opening the Home Front." *Reviews in American History* 8:3 (1980): 393–7.

Schiesl, Martin. "City Planning and the Federal Government in World War II: The Los Angeles Experience." *California History* 59:2 (April 1979): 126–43.

"Shoreline Development Study for Los Angeles." *American City, 59* (August 1944): 11.

Sitkoff, Harvard. "Racial Militancy and Interracial Violence in the Second War." *Journal of American History* 58:3 (December 1971): 661–81.

Smith, Alonzo and Taylor, Quintard. "Racial Discrimination in the Workplace: A Study of Two West Coast Cities During the 1940s." *The Journal of Ethnic History, 8* (Spring 1980): 35–54.

Spaulding, Charles B. "Housing Problems of Minority Groups in Los Angeles County." *Annals of the American Academy of Political and Social Science, 248* (November 1946): 220–5.

Tuck, Ruth D. "Behind the Zoot Suit Riots." *Survey Graphic, 32* (August 1943): 313–6+.

"The Undiscovered City." *Fortune, 39* (June 1949): 76–83.

Viehe, Fred W. "The Recall of Mayor Frank L. Shaw: A Revision." *California History* 59:4 (1980–1981): 290–305.

Weinberg, Sidney. "What to Tell America, the Writers Quarrel in OWI." *Journal of American History, 55* (June 1968): 73–89.

Zierer, Clifford M. "Hollywood, World Center of Motion Picture Production." *Annals of the American Academy of Political and Social Science, 254* (November 1947): 12–7.

Unpublished Materials

Carson, Clay. (comp.) "The Minority Population in Los Angeles, 1860–1960." Survey Research Center, University of California, Los Angeles, 1971. [Mimeographed.]

"Carnegie–Myrdal Study" [of Conditions in Los Angeles in 1940.] Urban League Papers, Special Collections, University of California, Los Angeles.

Fuss, Oscar. "Paper on Mexican–American Problems in Los Angeles." Los Angeles County Grand Jury, 1942.

Hoijer, Harry. "The Problem of Crime Among the Mexican Youth of Los Angeles." Los Angeles: Los Angeles County Grand Jury, 1942.

Holton, Karl. "Delinquency in Wartime." Los Angeles: County Probation Office, 1942.

Los Angeles County Grand Jury. *Minutes*, 1942.

Los Angeles County Grand Jury. "Report of the Special Committee on Problems of Mexican–American Youths." Los Angeles: County Grand Jury, October, 1942.

"Transcript of Hearing Conducted by Carey McWilliams, Chief, State Division of Immigration and Housing, on Importation of Negro Labor to California." McWilliams Collection, University of California, Los Angeles, July 14, 1942.

Government Documents

Fair Employment Practices Committee, Final Report. Washington, DC, 1947.

Los Angeles. Board of Harbor Commissioners. *Annual Report: For the Fiscal Year Beginning July 1, 1946 and Ending June 30, 1947*.

Los Angeles. *Mayor*. Los Angeles Yearbook 1940–1941. [*1940, Your City at Work*.] [*1941, Your City Geared to Defense*.]

Los Angeles. Transportation Engineering Board. *Report of Traffic and Transportation Survey*. Los Angeles: Citzen's Transportation Survey Committee, 1940.

Los Angeles Chamber of Commerce. *Southern California and National Defense*. Los Angeles: Chamber of Commerce, 1940.

Los Angeles Citizens' Committee on Parks, Beach, and Recreational Facilities. *Parks, Beaches and Recreational Facilities for Los Angeles County*. Los Angeles, 1945.

Los Angeles County. Chief Administrative Officer. *Capital Projects Program, 1945–1946 and Future Years*. Los Angeles, 1945.

Los Angeles County Chamber of Commerce, Industrial Department. *Collection of Eight Studies on the Industrial Development of Los Angeles County*. Los Angeles Chamber of Commerce, n.d.

Los Angeles County Probations Office. Robert H. Scott. *Summary of Recommendations and Progress to Date of the Special Committee on Older Youth Gang Activity in Los Angeles and Vicinity, Statistical Report of Juvenile Delinquency Among Children of Latin–American Ancestry*. December 28, 1942.

Los Angeles County War Services Corp. *Final Report*. Los Angeles: Los Angeles County, 1945.

U.S. Army. Western Defense Command and Fourth Army, Final Report–Japanese Evacuation from the West Coast. Washington, DC, 1943.

U.S. Bureau of the Census. *Historical Statistics of the United States*, 2 vols. Washington, DC, 1976.

U.S. Bureau of the Census. *Historical Statistics of the United States, 1789–1945*. Washington, DC, 1952.

U.S. Bureau of the Census. Sixteenth Census (1940). *Census of the Population: 1940, Characteristics of the Population*, Volume II. Washington, DC: Government Printing Office, 1942.

U.S. Bureau of the Census. Seventeenth Census (1950). *Census Tract Statistics: Los Angeles, California and Adjacent Area: Selected Population and Housing Characteristics*, Volume III, Chapter 28. Washington, DC: Government Printing Office, 1952.

U.S. Bureau of the Census. "Characteristics of the Population, Labor Force, Families, and Housing, Los Angeles Congested Production Area: April, 1944." Seris CA–3, No.5.

U.S. Bureau of the Census. "Wartime Changes in Population and Family Characteristics, Los Angeles Congested Production Area: April, 1944." Series CA–2, No. 5. Mimeographed, August 4, 1944.

U.S. Congress. House. 78th Cong., 1st sess., Subcommittee on Congested Areas, Subcommittee of Committee on Naval Affairs, *A Report on the Los Angeles–Long Beach Area*, Report #163. Washington, DC, 1944.

U.S. Congress. House. 78th Cong., 2d sess., House, Subcommittee on Congested Areas, Subcommittee of Committee on Naval Affairs, *A Report of the Congested Areas Subcommittee of Committee on Naval Affairs*, Report #144. Washington, 1944.

U.S. Office of War Information. *Pacific Coast Attitudes Toward the Japanese Problem*. Washington, DC, 1942.

U.S. War Department. *Japanese Evacuation from the West Coast*. Washington, DC, 1946.

Congressional Hearings

U.S. Congress. House. 77th Cong., 2d sess., Select Committee Investigating National Defense Migration Pursuant to House Resolution #113.

Hearings (34 parts). Washington, DC: Government Printing Office, 1940–1942.

U.S. Congress. House. 78th Cong., 1st sess., Subcommittee of Committee on Naval Affairs. *Hearings on Congested Areas* (8 parts). Washington, DC: Government Printing Office, 1944.

U.S. Congress. Senate. 76th Cong., 2d sess., Special Committee to Investigate the National Defense Program. *Hearings* (Parts 1–43). Washington, DC: Government Printing Office, 1941–1947.

U.S. Congress. Senate. 76th Cong., 2d sess., Subcommittee of Committee on Military Affairs. *Hearings on Motion Picture Industry*. Washington, DC: Government Printing Office, 1942.

U.S. Congress. Senate. 77th Cong., 1st sess., Special Committee Investigating the National Defense Program. *Hearings Before a Special Committee Investigating the National Defense Program*. Washington, DC: Government Printing Office, 1941–1948.

U.S. Congress. Senate. 78th Cong., 1st sess., Subcommittee of the Committee on Military Affairs, *Hearings on Labor Shortages in the Pacific Coast and Rocky Mountain States*. Washington, DC: Government Printing Office, 1943.

U.S. Congress. House. 78th Cong., 1st sess., Committee on the Merchant Marine and Fisheries, *Production in Shipbuilding Plants*. Hearings. (4 parts) Washington DC: Government Printing Office, 1943.

Theses and Dissertations

Anderson, Ernest Frederick. "The Development of Leadership and Organization Building in the Black Community of Los Angeles from 1900 through World War II." Ph.D. dissertation, University of Southern California, 1976, pp. 308.

Baisden, Richard N. "Labor Union in Los Angeles Politics." Ph.D. dissertation, University of Chicago, 1958.

Bottles, Scott L. "The Making of the Modern City: Los Angeles and the Automobile, 1900–1950." Ph.D. dissertation, University of California, Los Angeles, 1984.

Browell, R. Kenneth. "Some Social Implications of the National Defense Problem in Los Angeles County, with Special Reference to Three Typical Communities." Master's thesis, Claremont Graduate School, 1941.

Browne, Michael. "Survey of the Hollywood Entertainment Film During the War Years 1941–1943." Master's thesis, University of California, Los Angeles, 1951.

Burch, Edward A. "Attitudes of Employers Engaged in Manufacturing in the Los Angeles Area Relative to the Employment of Negroes." Master's thesis, University of Southern California, 1949.

Crimi, James E. "The Social Status of the Negro in Pasadena, California." Master's thesis, University of Southern California, 1941.

Darling, Kenneth Tuttle. "Controlled Manpower: Experiences of World War II; A Study of the Activities of the War Manpower Commission in the Los Angeles–Harbor Shipbuilding Industry." Master's thesis, University of Redlands, Redlands, CA, 1951.

DeGraaf, Lawrence B. "Negro Migration to Los Angeles, 1930–1950." Ph.D. dissertation, History, University of California, Los Angeles, 1962.

Domer, Marilyn. "The Zoot–Suit Riot: A Culmination of Social Tensions in Los Angeles." Master's thesis, Claremont Graduate School, 1955. 193 pp.

Dunkle, John R. "The Tourist Industry of Southern California: A Study in Economic and Cultural Geography." Master's thesis, University of California, Los Angeles, 1950.

Ferguson, Charles K. "Political Problems and Activities of Oriental Residents in Los Angeles and Vicinity." Master's thesis, University of California, Los Angeles, 1942.

Greer, Scott. "The Participation of Ethnic Minorities in the Labor Unions of Los Angeles County." Ph.D. dissertation, University of California, Los Angeles, 1962.

Harris, Cynthia H. "Little Tokyo of Los Angeles; March 1, 1937–August 17, 1949." Master's thesis, Claremont Graduate School, 1970.

Higins, Carla. "Art Collecting in the Los Angeles Area, 1910–1960." Ph.D. dissertation, University of California, Los Angeles, 1963.

Hopkinson, Shirley. "An Historical Account of the Evacuation, Relocation, and Resettlement of the Japanese in the United States, 1941–1946." Master's thesis, Claremont Graduate School, 1951.

Jackman, Jarrell C. "Exiles in Paradise: A Cultural History of German Emigrés in Southern California, 1933–1950." Ph.D. dissertation, University of California, Santa Barbara, 1977.

Lane, Robert Gerhart. "The Administration of Fletcher Bowron as Mayor of the City of Los Angeles." Master's thesis, University of Southern California, September 1954.

Leader, Leonard Joseph. "Los Angeles and the Great Depression." Ph.D. dissertation, History, University of California, Los Angeles, 1972.

O'Connor, George M. "The Negro and the Police in Los Angeles." Master's thesis, University of Southern California, 1955.

Penrod, Vesta. "Civil Rights Problems of Mexican-Americans in Southern California." Master's thesis, Claremont Graduate School, 1948.

Renov, Michael. "Hollywood's Wartime Woman: A Study of Historical-Ideological Determination." Ph.D. dissertation, University of California, Los Angeles, 1982.

Richards, Eugene S. "The Effects of the Negro's Migration to Southern California Since 1920 upon His Socio–Cultural Patterns." Ph.D. dissertation, University of Southern California, 1941.

Rothstein, Mignon. "A Study of the Growth of Negro Population in Los Angeles and Available Housing Facilities Between 1940 and 1946." Master's thesis, University of Southern California, 1950.

Sauberli, Harry A., Jr. "Hollywood and World War II." Master's thesis, University of Southern California, 1967.

Scott, Robin F. "The Mexican–American in the Los Angeles Area, 1920–1950: From Acquiescence to Activity." Ph.D. dissertation, University of Southern California, 1971.

Shinn, Richard D. "The Location of the Apparel Industry in Los Angeles." Master's thesis, University of Southern California, 1962.

Smith, Alonzo Nelson. "Black Employment in the Los Angeles Area." Ph.D. dissertation, University of California, Los Angeles, 1978.

Solomon, James Jones. "The Government Riots of Los Angeles, June 1943." Master's thesis, University of California, Los Angeles, 1969.

Sparks, Frank H. "The Location of Industry: An Analysis of Some of the Factors Which Have Affected the Location of Industry in Ten Southern Counties of California." Ph.D. dissertation, University of Southern California, 1941.

Tamaru, Takuji. "An Analysis of the Factors Which Have Influenced the Location of the Apparel Industry in Los Angeles." Master's thesis, University of Southern California, 1951.

Tipton, Gene B. "The Labor Movement in the Los Angeles Area During the Nineteen–Forties." Ph.D. dissertation, History, University of California, Los Angeles, 1953.

Tom, K. F. "The Participation of the Chinese in the Community Life of Los Angeles." Master's thesis, University of Southern California, 1944.

Unrau, Harlan D. "The Double V Movement in Los Angeles during the Second World War: A Study in Negro Protest." Master's thesis, History, California State University, Fullerton, 1971.

Utter, James W., Jr. "The Territorial Expansion of Los Angeles." Master's thesis, University of Southern California, 1946.

Wilburn, James R. "Social and Economic Aspects of the Aircraft Industry in Metropolitan Los Angeles During World War II." Ph.D. dissertation, History, University of California, Los Angeles, 1971.

Williams, Dean L. "Some Political and Economic Aspects of Mexican Immigration into the United States Since 1941; With Particular Reference to This Immigration in the State of California." Master's thesis, University of California, Los Angeles, 1950.

Williams, Dorothy S. "Ecology of Negro Communities in Los Angeles County: 1940–1959." Ph.D. dissertation, Sociology, University of Southern California, 1961.

Oral History

In Special Collections Division, University of California, Los Angeles: Borough, Reuben. University of California, Los Angeles, Oral History Project, Los Angeles, California.

In Special Collections Division, University of California, Los Angeles: Bowron, Fletcher. University of California, Los Angeles Oral History Project, Los Angeles, California.

In Special Collections Division, University of California, Los Angeles: Ford, John Anson. University of California, Los Angeles Oral History Project, Los Angeles, California.

In Special Collections Division, University of California, Los Angeles: McWilliams, Carey. University of California, Los Angeles Oral History Project, Los Angeles, California.

In Special Collections Division, University of California, Los Angeles: Poulson, Norris. University of California, Los Angeles Oral History Project, Los Angeles, California.

In Special Collections Division, University of California, Los Angeles: Story, Harold H. University of California, Los Angeles Oral History Project, Los Angeles, California.

Periodicals

Business Week, 1939–1945.

Commonweal, 1939–1945.

Fortune, 1939–1945.

New Republic, 1939–1946.

Newsweek, 1939–1945.

Security-First National Bank of Los Angeles. *Monthly Summary of Business Conditions in Southern California*, 1938–1948.

Time, 1939–1945.

Western City, 1939–1946.

Newspapers

California Eagle, 1939–1945.

Long Beach Telegram, 1939–1946.

Los Angeles Daily News, 1939–1946.

Los Angeles Examiner, 1939–1946.

Los Angeles Herald–Express, 1939–1946.

Los Angeles Times, 1939–1946.

Santa Monica Evening Outlook, 1939–1945.

Westwood Hills Press, 1939–1945.

Index